2-16

DISCARD

Building
Support Networks
for Schools

Building
Support Networks
for Schools

Patricia Jean Wagner

ABC-CLIO
Santa Barbara, California
Denver, Colorado
Oxford, England

Library of Congress Cataloging-in-Publication Data

Wagner, Patricia Jean.
    Building support networks for schools / Patricia Jean Wagner.
      p. cm.
    Includes bibliographical references and index.
    1. Communication in education—United States.   2. Social networks
—United States.   3. Interpersonal communication—United States.
    4. Community and school—United States.   I. Title.
    LB1033.5.W34   1991   370.19′31—dc20   91-32021

ISBN 0-87436-615-1

99 98 97 96 95 94 93 92   10 9 8 7 6 5 4 3 2 1 (paper)

ABC-CLIO, Inc.
130 Cremona Drive, P.O. Box 1911
Santa Barbara, California 93116-1911

This book is printed on acid-free paper ∞ .
Manufactured in the United States of America

For my mother, Esther D. Wagner,
and my husband, Leif Smith,
who made this possible

Contents

Preface

Peter J. McLaughlin, a nationally known corporate trainer and co-author (with James E. Loehr) of the best-selling book *Mentally Tough,* teaches an innovative series of workshops on fitness and self-esteem to school districts all over the United States, including Phoenix, Arizona; San Bernardino, California; and St. Louis, Missouri. Part of each workshop has to do with problem solving and risk taking, and he has had a chance to watch some of the country's top educators in action. A former high school and college teacher and coach, McLaughlin has observed school systems as a teacher, parent, and trainer. He states that some school system employees are not prepared to reach out to the business and professional communities for help. Even some decision makers, such as superintendents and principals, are hesitant to ask for assistance. "They need more enthusiasm for learning new ideas from other communities than the teacher and school community," McLaughlin notes.

Kimberley Taylor, former director of marketing and development for the nationally known Denver Children's Museum, is director of special projects for the Colorado State Library, which is under the Colorado State Board of Education. She agrees that many teachers and school media specialists don't reach out as much as they might. "Studies have shown that the leading reason worthy programs do not get funding and support is because the people involved don't ask," says Taylor, who recently secured a major corporate source to fund a project. The funder said that the reason Taylor got the grant was that she was the only one who came forward with an idea.

Another potential source of support for schools is the media. But how do you build rapport with the reporters and editors who can educate and influence the voters to support a bond issue, for example? Organizations do not think, see, listen, touch, or write letters to the editor; people who work in organizations, however, do all of these things. The trust between the organizations called the media and the organization called the school is really a relationship built up between teachers and administrators on one side and reporters and editors on the other.

Gloria Anderson, publisher of a community newspaper in Florida and an experienced reporter and editor for major daily papers, says that the time to build relationships with the media is *before* a crisis occurs. She explains that the element of trust must be built over a period of time.

Yet another source of support is parents and relatives of students. Many people would gladly volunteer to help if given the chance. But remember, in creating opportunities for family members to participate in school programs, you and others in your school need to be flexible. Are you ever tempted to complain about the unresponsiveness of parents to a request for help without first finding out their reasons? Chris Hobbs, a former art teacher and a parent in southern Wisconsin, received very different messages from the several school districts her three children have attended. While one district virtually ignored most of the parents, her most recent district has gone out of its way to make parents feel welcome, including holding a highly successful school fair run by a parent-teacher coalition. Hobbs advises that communication is the key.

Finding the right people to support a project or cause is not easy, particularly if you wait until you are up against a deadline to begin your search. Instead, build mutually useful relationships before the crisis stage. Begin with the individuals you know best— members of your family, friends, neighbors—and grow your network to include many people who are outside the boundaries of your profession. You can build a support system that you can count on for personal and professional help and information on everything from reducing stress to dealing with a difficult family member to moving up your career ladder.

The key terms here are *mutually useful.* Building useful relationships does not mean you must be a pushy or exploitive person, like the network builder who boasts that she never picks up a lunch tab. Compensation for someone's time, information, and resources rarely has to be monetary; truly effective networking is based on the fact that most people enjoy being useful.

Despite the negative publicity given to schools in recent years—or maybe because of it—many people in the larger community want to help. Most, however, don't know where to start. In your own district, what happens when someone contacts a school to volunteer time and resources? Your efforts to reach potential volunteers can have a positive "domino" effect in your school district. You do not have to start a new committee or spend precious funds for resources like computers and equipment. Of course, you need to invest time, but most of it will be in five- and ten-minute chunks. You also need to be aware of possibilities; for example, by talking to the policewoman you see in the grocery store, you can meet your need for a speaker on nontraditional careers for women. You also need to take some time to plan for future contacts. But you will be rewarded hundredfold for your investment.

What Is a Network?

The practical definition of what scholars call a "social network" is simple: a set of relationships built on information and idea exchange for mutual benefit. Some authors incorporate information about "affinity bonds" and "kinship links" in their definitions of a network. Others maintain that a network is any exchange of information, goods, or services between two or more people, even if the delivery of the information is one-sided and no personal contact occurs among the recipients of that information.

In management theory and practice circles, the word *network* has a glamorous cast and carries with it the promise of democracy and mutual respect, of trust and equal access to information and other resources. Consequently, it pops up in the names of women's magazines, community education programs, library database systems, even dating services! However, in its brief lifespan as a term for a type of interactive human behavior and a designed structure with similar qualities, *network* also has generated mistrust and disappointment. Many so-called networks are only the old, familiar kinds of associations and organizations with new names. Similarly, the members of these "networks" measure their outreach efforts in terms of the number of brochures mailed, the number of meetings attended, and the number of offices held. All of these are worthy endeavors, but they can actually get in the way of useful network building.

How This Book Can Help

Some of the questions people have about building support networks include:

1. Where do I find people willing to give time and resources to my school? What do I have to do to convince them to help me? How do I approach them?

2. How much record keeping do I need to do? Do I have to set up a computer system?

3. Aren't these kinds of relationships exploitive and manipulative?

4. I have lots of friends and contacts, but I can never seem to find people to help me. Am I doing something wrong?

5. I already am a good networker. Why do I need a book to teach me something as natural as communicating with other people?

6. We already have a public affairs director at our school. Why should I add building such relationships to my list of duties?

7. Isn't this kind of behavior unprofessional? Aren't you asking me to be a salesperson?

8. I don't know anyone—how do I proceed?

This book is about how you can make the promise of the word *network* come true, by consciously creating and maintaining networks of support for your school and the community it serves. The book focuses on your opportunity and responsibility to build working relationships with people in your school building, including teachers, administrators, media specialists, support staff, and students. It will expand your awareness of people who might become part of your school's support network and how you can apply that awareness in your professional conduct. It details some of the crucial ways networks differ from other kinds of structures, such as business partnerships, libraries, clearinghouses, and service clubs, and shows you how to keep relationships alive and well whether or not they exist within a continuous formal structure.

If you are already successful at building support networks, this book can help you pinpoint what you are doing right and show you how to increase the efficiency and size of your networks. It can also teach you some tricks for polishing your communication and record-keeping skills. If you think of yourself as a rank beginner, you will find hundreds of tips for getting started, examples of successful network campaigns, and a sample workshop format and handout to adapt for your own programs. And, if you are concerned that building these types of relationships is a way of exploiting other people, you are in for a pleasant surprise. The basis for all network building is being useful to other people and creating the kinds of relationships that benefit both the individual and the community to the greatest extent possible.

Acknowledgments

Creating a book on network building starts, of course, with people. I began by sending out more than 100 letters to friends, family members, and clients, from teachers in California to parents in New England, asking for help. I wrote to former high school and college classmates, some of whom I have not seen or spoken with for decades. I talked to strangers at parties and to participants at my network-building workshops.

In response I received phone calls, letters, and visits from people from all over the country; some were fourth- and fifth-generation connections from strangers willing to share their ideas and experiences. Suggestions and assistance were offered by teachers, school administrators, freelance writers, psychologists, corporate trainers, parents, magazine editors, media specialists, computer specialists, university professors, directors of nonprofit organizations, and education activists. Many of these people are mentioned in this text; some have written books and articles that are cited in Appendix C.

Over the years I have conducted hundreds of workshops on network building and conflict resolution for school media specialists, librarians, teachers, professionals, and the general public. Notes from these workshops and the comments of participants generated many of the ideas in this book. I also thank clients of the Office for Open Network, the information service I run with my husband, Leif Smith. Sixteen years of trying to practice what I preach while observed by hundreds of expert network builders has been the best preparation for writing this book.

Special thanks to my friends in the library and education communities throughout the state of Colorado, particularly the directors and staffs of the library service systems, the Colorado State Library Resource Center, the Colorado State Department of Education, and, of course, the editors at ABC-CLIO, who first suggested this book. In particular, I value the honesty of school personnel and parents who shared with me their challenges, successes, and failures.

All of the examples used in this book, to the best of my knowledge, are true. In some cases, details have been changed and names have been deleted or changed to protect the anonymity of sources.

Building
Support Networks
for Schools

1

Understanding Network Building

"There is more to the obvious than is obvious."[1]

The surprise about network building is how much of it consists of the common-sense behavior used by any good communicator. When a group of school media specialists and teachers were asked what was the most useful information they would take back to their schools from a networking workshop, they responded:

"Talk and ask questions of people I have avoided."

"Listen more."

"Be more confident about what I have to offer."

"Break down barriers between a colleague and myself."

"Delegate more responsibilities to local authorities and co-workers."

"Continue to remember to take risks."

"Remember not to assume!"[2]

The remarkable characteristic of these comments is that so many in a group of well-educated, experienced professionals appreciated being reminded of the need to talk to people.

Network versus Archive

Many kinds of human behavior and organizations satisfy some of the criteria of successful network building. However, the differences are crucial and warrant attention. On the spectrum of information management, network building is at one end and archive building is at the other. The purest network activity is what happens when you are walking down a street and a stranger stops you for directions. You point out the landmarks, she thanks you, and you both go your separate ways. There is no written record of the transaction. You offer useful information to the stranger and receive, in turn, the warm glow of doing a good deed. No scorecard is kept, the encounter is brief, and the two parties don't even know each other. The relationship lasts only a moment, and both parties probably forget about it in a few hours. The goal was to fulfill a need, period.

The purest archival activity, on the other, might be typified by the last scene in the popular adventure movie *Raiders of the Lost Ark*. After surviving enormous dangers, the hero locates the original Ark of the Covenant and saves it from the villains. The ark is a prize of enormous power and religious significance, but the government puts it out of sight and out of reach in a huge warehouse, where it becomes part of a vast and immobile collection. The thick layer of dust on every object in the warehouse indicates that none of them have been touched for years. The goal in such an archive is simple storage; whoever collects the most, wins.

Most networks and archives are not this extreme, of course. For most networking, some kind of documentation is needed, if only to keep track of names and phone numbers. An information desk at a major airport, for example, has directories and maps to help both the staff behind the desk and the people they serve. On the other hand, the librarian or records manager in charge of the dustiest archives usually knows something about what is contained on the shelves. Following are some of the practical differences between networks and archives.

Relationships versus Documents

A network is based on the relationships among the people in the web, while an archive relies on documents. In this context, documents include any recorded information, from books and papers to computer databases and artwork. The more time spent collecting, cataloging, and retrieving information, the less time can be spent focusing on people.

Aging of information is a critical factor in data management. Systems that emphasize file cabinets filled with sheets of paper or bytes of electronic data can lead to accumulations of information that are no longer accurate or complete. One information broker made a humiliating mistake because she forgot to use her networks. She spent several weeks searching the library for information on private vocational schools for a client. After the client paid for the report, he decided to check out the school she recommended in person. Unfortunately, the school had closed its doors several weeks earlier.

This isn't to say that all old information is useless (or that all information becomes old within the space of a few weeks). Old directories can be valuable historical documents, and even if the information about a specific organization is no longer correct, the entry can lead you to current information. But by focusing more of your attention on people, particularly those at the cutting edge, you are more likely to be at the cutting edge yourself.

Load Distribution

Instead of reinventing the wheel many times over, a network builder finds people whose job or avocation is keeping track of a particular kind of information or solving a particular kind of problem. When you are building networks, who you know is at least as important as what you know or what documents you possess. The spirit of the network builder is exemplified in a conversation overheard at a gallery opening. A woman was being complimented on knowing "everyone in the city." She demurred politely, "I don't know everyone, but I know several people who do."

Cultivate your network of information gatherers through academic institutions, professional associations, publication staffs, and nonprofit organizations. Find someone with a great passion for collecting information on corporate funding sources for music education in your state and build a relationship with her, rather than trying to duplicate her vertical files. Instead of competing with the teacher who claims to have the definitive library on learning disorders in the county, praise the thoroughness of her collection and find a way to share in her information. Your network is bound to include people who specialize in acquiring certain kinds of information, such as how to build a toy library, how to run a successful alternative high school in a public school system, or how to teach science to grade-school children. A good network lets you call on your supply of experts for information on a specific topic, rather than you trying to collect it all yourself.

Many experts use networks to keep track of what is happening in their own fields. Jennifer Burnham trains professionals in government and private agencies to deal with the challenges of identifying and caring for children with physical, emotional, and mental handicaps. An innovator in the field of respite care and special needs child care, she relies on various colleagues to keep her up to date. When she has a question, she can tap into her primary local network, which consists of about 50 people with whom she has excellent rapport and feels comfortable "just calling up." She also has a much smaller primary national network of about a half-dozen people.

Building relationships with experts allows you to take advantage of different archives, different points of view, and different cataloging techniques. For example, you might have several contacts with performance artists who specialize in working with children. Each artist is considered an expert in theater education. Each belongs to the same professional associations and subscribes to the same journals. But the books they collect, the meetings they attend, and the theories they apply in their work are quite different. By using these artists to keep track of information in the field for you, you have the advantage of several different minds filtering and processing overlapping sets of information. If you relied only on your own resources, you would miss the synergy of opinions and inputs that a network creates.

Active versus Static

Networks are fluid; they are maps of relationships that can change frequently. The activities of the participants fuel the relationships. An archive is frozen; any flow of information is predictable and usually is one-way. A network resembles an old-fashioned market day, with thousands of transactions happening at once. By contrast, with an archive the librarian or cataloger may be the only person authorized to give out information.

In a traditional organization, the formulas for interaction often are scripted to promote "efficiency" and "order." The chairperson rules, and communication is focused on supporting organizational goals. Conceivably, one can be a part of such an organization for a long time and do nothing more than pay dues. At a network meeting, however, official business is conducted as quickly and as painlessly as possible so that information can be exchanged among members to further each person's goals. In some groups, everyone takes a turn speaking, while in others people talk informally as the need or desire arises. Those who do not participate actively are eventually ignored; in some network organizations, active participation is a requirement of membership.

Collecting Clues versus Full Text Searches

In a network, most of the information the participants collect and exchange is in the form of "pointers" or clues to people, projects, other networks, and even archives. A network builder is more likely to keep a phone number than an entire file on an organization. An archivist, on the other hand, collects any piece of paper that is connected with the organization.

As a result, network builders can keep an amazing array of information in a relatively compact space. A list of 100 phone numbers might lead to 1,000 projects and 10,000 people. The archive builder provides full texts and must spend more time taking care of the vast store of information. Consequently, archive builders are often tied to a single office or building. Tools such as CD-ROM storage and online computer databases blur the distinction between network builders and archivists, but it is likely that the network builder needs fewer pages to get at the same data.

The Need for Balance

Archivists keep crucial records and know how to deal with warehouses of information so that the treasures are not lost forever. They do the difficult job of gathering and cataloging information, of creating structures that don't have to be re-created every day. Network builders are notoriously sloppy about record keeping; likewise, networks are notorious for having participants working simultaneously on a dozen identical projects. Both kinds of people are needed; both kinds of institutions are necessary. The problem is that there are fewer models for successful network building as opposed to constructing archives and more hierarchical structures.

The Five Rules of Networking

The network model is not new; it borrows from the wisdom of a dozen disciplines. However, people who stray too far from its ideal often find themselves less effective.

The First Rule: Be Useful and Let Others Be Useful to You

Networking is a dance based on the exchange of information. It is a process with no designated "givers" as opposed to "takers." Everyone has the potential to be useful, no matter what their status, age, or experience. Everyone also has the potential to receive help, regardless of the balance in their bank account or how many initials appear after their name.

The attitude that each person has potential both to offer and to receive creates a special bond of humanity among those who take it to heart. If you believe that each person you meet might be the one who can solve a problem or at least point you toward the solution, you tend to treat everyone you meet with respect and interest. You listen carefully to what they have to say and you ask questions. Because your attentiveness is genuine, those you meet are likely to respond in kind.

When you are surrounded by people who can be useful to you, the resources at your disposal increase. You can turn to more people for answers and suggestions. You have more room professionally to experiment and take risks; a failure is not as disastrous when other people are available to take up the slack. A network acts as a safety net—you do not have to be perfect, and you do not have to do it all yourself. By the same token, if you believe that you have the potential to be useful to everyone in some way, you are less likely to be intimidated by the rich, powerful, and famous. You are more likely to be proud of your accomplishments and the things you know.

During workshops on network building, participants learn to think in terms of exchanging, rather than giving and taking. Some people know the lesson already; others have a hard time moving out of one role or the other. But once most of a group gets the idea, the transformation is magical. The room is filled with people talking one-on-one or in small groups about whatever is most important to them, from school bond issues to trying to meet a mortgage payment.

Principals and administrators can benefit in such a setting as much as student aides. One state board of education had all of its employees participate in a two-hour network workshop instead of their normal staff meeting. Soon the building was filled with pairs and trios of people, vigorously expounding on ideas, swapping phone numbers, and trading tips on work and personal matters. Into the midst of the noise strolled the state commissioner of education. Although he had been warned to expect something different, the look on his face was priceless. A few of the participants smiled at him in greeting, but no one broke away from their conversations to talk with him. He watched for a while, until he was drawn into his own eager exchange. Some of the participants later reported that it was the most useful staff meeting they had been to in years.

The Importance of Reciprocity

Thinking about being useful and letting others be useful to you puts every transaction on equal ground. Using the principles of networking, if you are a teacher talking with a parent about a student who doesn't like to study, you abdicate the role of "expert" educator. Instead, you treat both the parent and the student as equal partners in an exchange where you pool your combined information, experience, training, and wisdom to solve the problem.

At conferences, the amount of time spent swapping ideas will become as crucial as that spent listening to the designated speakers. In building partnerships with other institutions, a knowledge of networking leads you to continually ask yourself and others: "Who else can contribute? Who else can we learn from? Who else can we serve?"

The first few times you try a new behavior, it can feel a little awkward. Network building is no exception. Some neophytes will demand to be useful immediately, although it is obvious that not every exchange is an equal transaction. The attitude is what counts—genuine interest in the other person, sincere thanks, and an offer to reciprocate in some way, even if the actual exchange is never completed.

Network building in its purest form is the exchange of intangibles, but small favors can build a bridge to future, more complex exchanges. What is offered does not have to be complicated or fancy. Mailing some letters, picking up a book at the library, writing a letter of reference, passing on news of a great sale, or listening sympathetically to a sad story are all examples of the most basic form of networking.

The Second Rule: Maintain a Balance between Giving and Taking

The cardinal rule of successful theater is simple: Don't bore the audience. The same rule applies to networks, except that in this case avoiding boredom means being able to maintain a balance that keeps you from either overwhelming your network contacts or burning out yourself. It is surprisingly easy for otherwise intelligent and interesting people to violate this rule—in fact, people who are the most conscientious about their jobs are the most likely to do so. Here are descriptions of three practices that can severely damage network relationships. All three mistakes are rooted in a disregard for or a misunderstanding of reciprocity.

Overwhelming—Giving Too Much

Kathleen Cain, a researcher and librarian at Front Range Community College in Westminster, Colorado, writes and teaches about building networks in schools. She warns against undermining the independence of students and faculty by doing too much for them (and burning yourself out in the process).

Network building focuses on short notes, brief conversations, and quick asides. Many professionals are prone to give too much information. The key is to provide the minimal number of clues a person needs to accomplish whatever she is trying to do—point her to the hardware store, don't stop to dig a foundation for her house. The best way to avoid overloading another person with information is to limit the amount of data and/or the number of contacts. It also helps to ask people to get back to you and tell you about how they used your information—this can help you decide what and how much information to give out in the future.

If you are the one asking for help, give your contact just enough information for them to understand your situation, so that they can help you and get back to whatever they were doing as quickly as possible.

Exploiting—Taking Too Much

Only a tiny percentage of people who use networks do so to exploit others. However, the fear of imposing on others is a major reason professionals hesitate to pick up the phone and ask a friend or stranger for assistance. If you are concerned about draining the people with whom you share information and contacts in your own networks, you can learn to balance your exchanges so that the chance of mutual burnout is less likely:

1. Begin conversations by asking if this is a good time to talk; if it isn't, find out when would be a better time.

2. Find out the best and worst times for calling your favorite contacts, and pass that information on to others. For example, is Sue a morning person or an evening person? Does she have young children at home? Is Friday her family's favorite television night? Is she on a project deadline?

3. With professionals and business people who usually charge for their services, clarify how they will deal with people you send to them. Are they willing to spend 10 minutes on the phone giving free advice, or should everyone you send expect to pay full price? You may need to renegotiate these agreements at frequent intervals.

4. Learn to ask for information succinctly.

5. Ask for one contact at a time, and tell the person giving you the information that you will let her know how the connection worked.

6. Do your homework before you call, write, or visit so you don't request information that can be more easily obtained in a document. This is especially important when contacting well-known experts, who are frequently asked to give two-minute summaries of their most famous works. Is it any wonder that some famous people, when asked for advice, snarl, "Why don't you buy my book? The information you want is in Chapter Three." Every author has a story about a request from a student to write back with "everything you know" on the subject of their expertise, often to help the student finish a term paper.

Refusing To Ask for Help

Some people can take pleasure only in giving. They give advice and information and enjoy their role as the person who solves their friends' problems. After a while, however, they drive away people who enjoy the reciprocal nature of network building.

Ironically, people who are most often identified by their peers as "networkers" are wonderful givers, but not good takers. They unintentionally promote the image of network building as something that "strong" people do for the "weak." In the teaching profession, this kind of relationship resembles the image of the instructor as someone who pours knowledge into the receptive brains of students. The mutual respect and appreciation are

11

missing. If you have problems asking for help, it is important to work at letting others be useful:

1. Be quiet once in a while and let other people solve the problems of the world.

2. Cultivate the habit of asking other people for help, even if the requests are small.

3. Admit it when you are wrong or you don't know the answer to someone's question.

The Third Rule: Listen

Network communication, as was mentioned above, should be a dance between two people. Sometimes one partner leads and dominates; in fact, he or she might lead almost all of the time. Networkers are notorious for talking too much. The problem with this is that true networking requires reciprocity. The person who is always talking rarely has a chance to receive, and the listener rarely has the opportunity to be useful. This type of "exchange" is very common in schools—one study cited by Gary Bergreen in *Coping with Difficult Teachers* (New York, 1988) found that most teachers feel uncomfortable in classroom situations where they ask a question followed by more than three seconds of silence.

Listening is a skill that everyone in the helping professions, including teaching, counseling, and librarianship, learns. Here are a few reminders about how to apply the same lessons to relationships with your colleagues and members of your school community:

1. Allow for silence.

There is a real pleasure at being able to sing out the information that will solve someone's problem. Some people don't even wait for the other person to finish the request; they step on the last words with their solution. The next time you have a conversation with someone, allow for a silence between their last words and your reply. Think about what they said, and allow them to add more. You are likely to hear valuable information. In some cultures, these kinds of thoughtful pauses are the norm. Even if it is not part of your upbringing to allow for a breather between monologues, most people appreciate the pause.

2.   Consciously listen to the person instead of planning your answer while they talk.

When you are listening to someone, are you listening to what they are saying? Do you pay attention to how they say it and what part of it is the most important to them? Do you listen for the parts you don't understand? Or are you someone who only listens for when the other person stops for a breath, so you can jump in and take over the conversation? In surveys of employees concerning their biggest complaints, "not being listened to by the boss" is usually ranked first. How could the atmosphere in your school be changed if people consciously listened to each other, without glancing at the clock, fidgeting, or breaking in with their own interpretation of the problem?

3.   Practice listening.

In this exercise, find a quiet place where you and a partner can sit comfortably and look at each other for about 30 minutes. During the first 10 minutes of the exercise, you talk and your partner must listen without saying a word. If you have nothing to say, you must sit still, but the other person cannot talk to fill the silence. During the second 10 minutes, switch roles: you listen silently and your partner talks. Then spend 10 minutes talking together about what happened. This is a useful exercise to use at staff meetings and as part of training programs for collaborative projects.

4.   Listen as if you never heard the information before.

People who know each other from working together on a daily basis easily fall into routines. You know what the other person is going to say before she opens her mouth. Conversations become rote, and even arguments begin to sound as if they were rehearsed. The network builder tries to listen to each conversation as if new information is being provided every time. The old words are examined for new meanings like the text of a familiar but well-loved poem. This attitude, which one network builder described as "looking for the gold," can improve the tone of every conversation and lead to new insights during periods of conflict.

5.   Listen to people you don't agree with.

Some network builders are wise enough to seek useful information specifically from people they disagree with to get a different perspective on the problems at hand. They purposely cultivate a whole set of unlikely resource persons to incorporate into their existing networks. The curmudgeon or cynic is valued for his or her critical eye. The person of opposing political beliefs keeps the network builder from falling prey to "group think." And persons of different cultures provide valuable feedback about the assumptions the network builder has made regarding his or her own behavior and opinions. Seeking out people who are unlike yourself in significant ways can improve both the diversity and the usefulness of your network.

The Fourth Rule: Ask Questions

Asking questions is a lost art. Students in high school and college learn debating techniques, in which one side wins and the other side loses. Disputes in the public arena are polarized into two points of view of cartoon simplicity. Adults express opinions to each other; there is agreement, indifference, or dissent, but rarely true discussion.

In network building, knowing how to ask questions is a special kind of service you can offer another person. To be interested enough to want more information is a compliment in most circumstances. Here are four kinds of questions, for better or worse, that people ask:

1.   Questions that punish

Obviously, these are not the kind of questions to use in your network building. But you hear them in public and private conversations too often not to realize they are part of how people communicate with each other. Ask yourself if you use these:

"What are you, nuts or something?"

"How can you say something like that?"

"Only people who don't care about the education of the children of this city could make a statement like that. And you agree with him?"

"Why did you let this happen?"

"Why don't you speak up? Are you deaf?"

People who ask such questions need to be a little more compassionate and a little less hasty about judging others' intentions.

2.   Questions that elicit information

These kinds of questions are the most valuable in the network builder's arsenal. The ability to find more information in a shorter period of time is part of the attraction of being in a network. Network building isn't just about whom you know, but about being able to find out what they know:

> "How do you know that is true?"
> "How did you learn that information?"
> "Can you tell me more about that?"
> "How did you come to that conclusion?"
> "What is your best guess about the situation?"
> "If you did have an answer, what would it be?"

3.   Questions that are brave

What are the secret questions that worry you about your work, your school, your community? These are the concerns that eat into people's self-confidence and make it hard for them to accomplish their tasks. But the truth is that you are not alone. Many of your colleagues and many of the participants in your networks probably share the same concerns:

> "Why is the emperor naked?"
> "Why are we naked?"
> "Why are we spending the money on this project?"
> "Why are there not more women, Native Americans, parents, farmers, teachers, principals, students, religious leaders, etc., in this room?"
> "Does anyone besides me think we made a mistake?"
> "Can you forgive me?"

4.   Questions that lead people to come up with their own answers

One of the highest compliments you can receive as a network builder is for someone to tell you that she came up with the answer herself and that all you did was ask the right questions. There is no public praise for being able to draw a solution out of the person who had the problem in the first place, but it is immensely gratifying.

This kind of question asking is a fine art, like tying a fancy fishing fly. It is delicate work and requires a light touch. Some of the following questions can be used successfully in most information situations. Asking these kinds of questions can also save you from making irrelevant suggestions:

"What have you tried before?"

"Why do you think it didn't work?"

"What would be the most useful thing I can do for you?"

"Can you think of any limits or restrictions I should know about before I answer your question?"

"What have been your worst experiences with the school?"

"Is there anyone you do not want to talk to about this problem?"

"If I weren't here, what would you do?"

The Fifth Rule: Don't Assume

The biggest assumption that the network builder must guard against is that only certain people can be useful in certain situations. We live in a culture where change is the rule. Every time you change, you add another node to your network. Every life contains milestones that can open doors to new networks of people and opportunities. For children and adolescents, such milestones include acquiring a new brother or sister, moving to a new neighborhood or school, taking up a hobby, taking a special vacation, or going to work in the family business. Events during college and young adulthood can include going away to school, starting a new job, and getting married. And adults encounter such milestones as divorce or remarriage, job changes, travel, professional triumphs and failures, and dealing with terminal illness or death.

Every life change creates new opportunities for learning. When you consider that most adults, and many children, have gone through numerous such changes, you come to realize the richness and diversity of every person's networks. The probability that someone has the answer to your question, or is part of a network that includes someone with the answer, is thus very high indeed.[3]

Imagine, as you walk down the halls of your school, that each adult represents the knowledge of hundreds of other adults, and each child, the knowledge of dozens of other adults and children. Even a small school harbors enormous possibilities. Nevertheless, it is easy to fall into the trap of looking only for the "right" people with whom to build your networks. The successful network builder remembers the first rule of networking and assumes that everyone can be useful.

The Challenge of Building Networks in Schools

The problem with applying network building to school reform is that almost all of the structures being suggested to create better communication within the schools, and between schools and their communities, are not networks. The appearance of network building is painted onto traditional institutions, and the old hierarchical structures are preserved and, in some cases, jealously guarded. For example:

The well-publicized parent-teacher councils in one midwestern city that held all of their meetings during the day, so that working parents could not attend.

The newsletter on school volunteer programs that was sent to every homeowner in an entire district but that failed to include information on how the recipients could participate, or even a phone number to call.

The statewide conference in a large western state to deal with the dropout problem from a community perspective; the special target for help was minority students. Of the more than 100 people invited to the planning meeting, only two were minorities. Everyone else was a Caucasian, middle-class teacher or school district employee.

The dozens of partnership meetings, conventions, Parent-Teacher-Student Associations (PTSAs), accountability councils, and coalitions that leave no time for significant membership interaction and devote few resources to asking the people they serve what they want.

In each of these cases, based on real events in school communities around the country, the intention to make positive change is sincere. The addition of network building that allows people to exchange, rather than just "give" or just "take," could improve the results of many well-intentioned efforts.

Notes

1. Spoken by the fictional character Hanmer Grant in an unpublished

manuscript, *The Road to Perinel,* by Leif Smith. The author likens building networks to the most basic practices of human intellectual and spiritual exploration.

2. Written comments collected from school librarians who participated in the author's network-building workshops during 1990.

3. See Appendix C for a selection of theory books on networking that cite a number of studies about how closely knit people on Earth really are.

---- 2 ----

Characteristics of Successful
Network Builders

Perhaps this is your image of a "super network builder": someone who is too busy to talk, too busy even to think. Her briefcase overflows with yellowing newspaper clippings and old newsletters. Phone message slips sit in mounds on her desk, on the front seat of her car, and on her kitchen counter. She always carries a datebook; by March the cover already has become frayed and the year, stamped in gold on the front, has mostly worn away.

At work, students and staff members assail her with requests and reminders: "Did you find the article you promised to clip?" "Are you going to the meeting on community safety?" "Can you locate three more volunteers for the career fair?" At home, her phone never stops ringing, her refrigerator is empty, and her dining room table is covered with unanswered letters, unpaid bills, and unread professional journals. She goes to the right community meetings, subscribes to the best educational magazines, and has the phone numbers of all of the most important people on the school board. Her life is a blur of activities and information. Friends tell her she is the best "networker" they know, and they rely on her for help in solving their problems.

Unfortunately this "network builder" has no time for a personal life. And, despite all the meetings and newsletters, she doesn't seem to have a handle on solving any of the problems facing her institution. Her reputation for effective follow-through is tarnished because she is taking on too many activities. Colleagues hesitate to ask her for help because they are never allowed to reciprocate, or they refuse to work on her projects because they have burned out due to her abuse of their services.

Such frenzied activity is not what network building is all about. People who tend to see network building as "another thing to do" may define it only in terms of alliances within formal organizations and equate it with long, boring meetings, rather than with the exchange of useful ideas over the phone. For the teacher who feels overwhelmed, the prospect of building a support network might sound suspiciously like having to serve on another committee or answer the demands of another special interest group, all without any personal reward.

By contrast, successful networkers see network building as a way of delegating work and allowing themselves more time and energy for their classes. A superintendent of a unified district in the Midwest makes it a point to attend community organization meetings and activities, not to participate officially, but rather to keep in touch with parents and community leaders. An elementary school teacher who moonlights as a clown says her contacts outside the school system give her perspective in her life and the energy to deal with the stress of her job. And a community organizer who works with low-income families on issues relating to gangs and drugs sees her ability to build alliances with others as a way to reach more people without burning herself out.

Being good at building networks means being good at communicating what you want from other people, and getting it. It means being able to offer assistance without becoming another victim of burnout. It means understanding how to use basic communication skills to build support for yourself and your institution.

Understanding Different Styles of Communication

Hilmar Jensen is a soft-spoken history teacher who has taught at the secondary and college levels in the Boston area for many years. He does not think of himself as extroverted, but he has been successful in inviting prominent members of the community into his classroom. He likes to make the history of the civil rights movement come alive for his students with the presence of experienced activists, and he is willing to share his classroom with other speakers. He seeks out speakers by talking with colleagues and friends about possible contributors. It helps, of course, to be teaching amidst the academic riches of the Boston area; he gets the names of many of his prospects from articles in local journals and magazines.

Jensen is most comfortable writing letters. In fact, when he is looking for a speaker, he would rather write a letter to a stranger than call on a friend, because, he says, he won't feel rejected if a stranger turns him down. (Although he feels shy because he rarely, if ever, has any money to offer his guests, most of the time people say yes, he says.) Jensen has learned how to add relevancy and excitement to his classes by reaching out to the community in a way he finds comfortable.

As Hilmar Jensen's experience shows, people need not be extroverts to be good communicators or good network builders. Jan Prince, a communication consultant, works with government employees, teachers, and business people. She says all individuals have different ways of gathering and responding to information; there are no formulas. By learning your own style of communicating, you can gain a better understanding of how other people deal with information and people. Then, she says, you won't be as likely to feel insulted if someone does not return a phone call or to assume the other person is not interested if she doesn't answer a letter.

The Three Communication Styles

You can use the following simple model to understand how you communicate and why it is easier for you to communicate with some people than with others.[1] The model outlines three basic styles of communication: visual, auditory, and kinetic. Most people use all three, but for any given individual one style tends to dominate. Understanding your own and others' communication styles can help you pinpoint why some of your attempts at communication go awry.

The Visual Orientation

The visually oriented person feels most comfortable communicating by means of the written word or pictures. A predominantly visual person is most likely to send a letter, post a note on a bulletin board, or feel the need for a visual record. For these people, information is most usable when it is written down or is in some kind of visual form, like a graph or chart.

Visuals tend to have well-organized Rolodexes and databases, and they adore modern technologies such as fax machines and electronic mail. Their main flaw as network builders is a tendency to flood colleagues with too much paper. They can fall into the trap of measuring success by the number of printed words they gather, rather than by the effectiveness of their relationships with people.

The Auditory Orientation

The auditory person feels most comfortable communicating by means of the spoken word. Auditory people spend hours on the phone and often leave elaborate messages on other people's answering machines. They prefer calling people to invite them to a meeting instead of mailing out invitations. Written records make auditories impatient; they would rather tape-record meetings instead of writing notes. Their idea of a useful network format is a phone tree.

Auditory people are the network builders with the best response time in a crisis; in fact, they pride themselves on being able to spend the least amount of time rounding up the most people to help on any given project. Their main flaw is a tendency to spend too much time talking and not enough time documenting what they have done.

The Kinetic Orientation

Kinetically oriented people need to be physically in touch with someone to be able to communicate. Unless they are face-to-face with the person they are talking with, they suspect they are somehow missing important information. Kinetics are the ones most likely to call a meeting to resolve a problem, and they spend a lot of professional and social time visiting people. They enjoy groups, and their network building is based on maintaining long-term relationships with colleagues and friends.

The kinetic style of networking resembles that of the old-fashioned political worker, whose network is really an extension of the family. Kinetics love parties and events, handshaking and kissing babies. Their networks last forever. Their main flaw is that their networking style, while extremely effective and able to build long-lasting connections, is limited by their ability to meet people in person. They are most comfortable with people they already know, and unless they have met someone in person at a conference, they typically do not take the time to call or write.

Which style is best? The answer, of course, is all three, depending on the people involved and the situation. Each style has its own strengths and limitations. The visual orientation is wonderful for people who swap newspaper clippings and academic papers; it is less useful when there is a deadline that precludes using the mail and requires communicating by telephone. The kinetic orientation builds strong alliances among diverse community groups, particularly among people who do not share the same language, but the success of the kinetic communicator can be limited by the need to meet with others in person. And the auditory orientation, despite its universal appeal in the age of voice mail and suitcase phones, can embroil the network builder in an endless game of phone tag.

Identifying Your Communication Style

Most participants in workshops on network building are immediately able to identify their dominant communication style. With a little thought, they are also able to identify the preferences of their colleagues, friends, and family. There are two simple ways to determine which style you prefer. The first is based on behavior. It is simple to determine your preferred style if you are a compulsive memo writer, a long-distance phone call addict, or someone who spends much of your free time over a cup of coffee with one or more friends. The second way is to notice the vocabulary you use to describe actions, ideas, and feelings:

1. A visually oriented person tends to use verbs such as *see, picture, portray, visualize,* and *paint.* For example:

    "Looks good to me!"
    "I can picture what you are trying to say."
    "Let me paint a picture of what I hope to achieve."

2. An auditory person tends to use verbs like *hear, ring, listen,* and *sounds:*

    "Sounds like a fine idea."
    "Did I hear that you want to increase the budget?"
    "This kind of curriculum rings a bell with me."

3. The kinetically oriented person uses feeling verbs, such as *understand, feel, touch, sense,* and *stand:*

    "I sensed you were uncomfortable at the meeting."

23

"Did you feel what I was trying to accomplish with the brochure?"

"I can't stand your behavior."

Once you come up with a likely premise, check it against the experience of friends, family, and colleagues. You may find out that you use one style more with one person than with another. You might also discover that the style you think you use is not the style other people believe you use.

Few people use only one style, so even if you are able to identify a dominant personal preference, you probably have some feel for the other two styles. Most importantly, you need to be able to respond to the personal preferences of others. The more competence you develop in each style, the more likely it is that you will receive responses to your various communications. The key, then, is not perfecting one style, but being flexible when it comes to other people's styles. Learning to use and be comfortable with all three methods increases your ability to build useful relationships.

The Importance of Flexibility

Timing is more than knowing that some people wake up cheerful or that others are confirmed "night owls." Timing refers to being sensitive to the rhythms of a person's workday. If you know that someone has had a recent disappointing experience or that he has trouble at home, you will avoid asking for information just before he must leave school to pick up a child from a doctor's appointment or face an unpleasant meeting with the principal.

Similarly, if you are a morning person, you don't have to limit your best relationships to other morning people. The best communicators can modify their timing, vocabulary, and appearance to suit the occasion and the audience, without violating their own standards. Begin by understanding more about yourself and your limitations as a communicator. Pick one limitation to work on and practice with a friend before trying your new skill with others in your network. For example, if you are an afternoon person, you might practice making one phone call each morning. Good communication is something you can practice and refine, and the limits you see and feel today are less rigid than you might think.

Community Organizer versus Network Builder

Some network builders pattern their tactics after those used by community organizers of the 1950s and 1960s. Using this model, they build working relationships based on the way people form emotional bonds during a battle against a common evil. For a public or community institution, this kind of model can be deadly. It works because it simplifies human disagreement into a moral battle between the "good us" and the "evil them." Some of the characteristics of this kind of neighborhood- or community-scale battle typify the kind of propaganda you read and hear when nations are at war. For example:

1. Our motives are always pure; their motives are always suspect.

2. We make mistakes because we are imperfect and human; they make mistakes because they intend evil and are somehow less than human.

3. We have the "good" people on our side; they have the"bad" people on their side.

4. We use derogatory language and slang to describe their people because we are accurately describing their despicable behavior; when they do the same thing, they are being inflammatory and slanderous.

5. We don't end the battle because we are proud; they don't give in because they are stubborn.

Contrast the above with the attitudes of network builders:

1. Network builders have high self-esteem. They do not have to be right every time and they regard the truth as more important than being perfect. They generally do not feel threatened if someone else has a different, even better, idea.

2. Network builders have a strong interest in diversity. For example, the Institute for Independent Education, Inc. in Washington, D.C., is a formal network of private minority schools in urban areas.[2] The single membership criterion embraces a diverse group of schools representing many cultural groups, educational philosophies, religious persuasions, and sizes.

3. The network builder considers the opposition as a potential source of assistance. Some individuals, because of their behavior or beliefs, are not likely to be at the top of your "call-up-and-say-hello" list. However, the best network builders are able to include in their networks people with different ideas and belief systems. Accepting that someone has an opposing point of view is not the same as supporting that person's opinion or agreeing with them.

The Three Kinds of Network Builders

There are three main approaches to building a useful network. The most effective networkers incorporate a mix of all three, depending on the circumstances. In each case, a positive attitude is the most important determinant for a successful outcome. If you assume that the people you are contacting will be cheerful and generous about swapping information, you are likely to be successful.

Building Rapport with Everyone:
The Universal Networker

Ferne Hoeft is an experienced and successful network builder who worked as a journalist and shared church work with her minister husband before becoming a secondary school English teacher. During her years of teaching, which netted national recognition for both her students and herself, she built strong alliances with her students, the administration of the school, and the greater community. Her ability to build trust and rapport came, she says, from her faith in the divine spark she sees in everyone. No one is excluded from her warmth and kindness, no matter what the person's station or role. She is the kind of teacher who engenders strong loyalty from her students because she treats them with respect.

Universal networkers regard every person they meet as a potential resource for advice and ideas, regardless of the person's education and social or professional status. Here are some characteristics of universal network builders:

1. They tend to be late for meetings because they are talking with someone in the hall.

2. Having a meal with them in a restaurant usually takes a while because they seem to know everyone in the room, including the host or hostess, the owner, and the waiters and waitresses.

3. They are likely to stop to help someone by the side of the road.

4. They know the secretaries as well as the executives.

Universal networkers smile at everyone and ask lots of questions. They tend to be sloppy network builders, in that they collect more information than they can ever use. However, they are least likely to run out of ideas.

Focusing Your Efforts:
The Efficient Network Builder

Many successful business-school and community-school partnership leaders fall into the category of the efficient network builder. Such people are well organized and disciplined and take a no-nonsense approach to their craft. Their network building connects powerful individuals and organizations, and they pride themselves on the important people who serve on their boards of directors.

The strength of efficient network builders is the ability to design strategies for engaging important people in their work. These network builders consider participation in their causes a sort of "noblesse oblige," and they are likely to serve on several community-based boards. They don't "waste time" with people who are unable to deliver, and they are extremely successful at applying political pressure to help their organizations and schools succeed. Like universal networkers, efficient networkers are easy to spot:

1. Conversations with them tend to be to the point, oriented to a particular result, and decisive; talking to them gives people the feeling that they are accomplishing something useful.

2. Their follow-through is usually excellent.

3. They are effective with a variety of organizations but are most likely to be comfortable working with the top people.

4. They have the best-looking address books.

The problem with efficient networkers is a tendency to subscribe to the "name tag" school of network building: they look at the title on someone's name tag, decide if that person is worth the trouble; if not, they move on. They accomplish a great deal, but their network building tends to be more selective and more oriented toward institutional models. People who are not part of an organization or an identifiable group in the community or who don't attend charitable events and public rallies tend to be invisible to the efficient networker.

Playing the Wild Card: The Adventurous Network Builder

Adventurous netwo1rk builders are the least efficient of the three types. They love to dream, plan impossible projects, call meetings for their latest schemes, and sit up late at all-night diners writing in their journals. One day they might be selling exotic jewelry picked up on a trip to Central America, and the next day you'll find them organizing a fair for a group of community activists. They have eclectic bags of acquaintances: corporate business persons, governors, jazz musicians, spiritualists, community activists, writers, and people they met on the bus. Adventurous networkers build relationships because they are fascinated with other people. The characteristics of these networkers include the following:

1. They are likely to bring the most interesting person to the staff party.

2. Their networking style is to walk up to strangers and ask their opinions about obscure philosophical questions.

3. They are likely to speak several languages, albeit poorly, and to have friends with whom they must converse via an interpreter.

Adventurous networkers build networks through their love of interesting people and are the least concerned about working relationships and measurable results.

The most successful network builders combine all three styles. They are universal in their ability to relate to everyone in their school community. They are efficient in designing the structures needed to keep their schools thriving and interacting with other institutions and organizations. And they are adventurous in reaching out to people who may be invisible because of status or cultural isolation from the mainstream.

Notes

1. Much of the information on the communication model is courtesy of Lara Amber Ewing and Jan Prince, both Denver-based communication consultants who work with individuals and institutions.
2. See Appendix C for more information about the institute and other national educational networks.

---- 3 ----

Mapping Networks and Network Generators

Every person lives in a web of multiple networks. Each employee of your school and each person in your greater school community is part of his or her own networks. When you identify the connections that give meaning to an individual's life, you can discover new avenues for rapport and trust. This chapter provides a discussion of the kind of networks that you and the people you want to reach might inhabit and an examination of the two main ways network relationships are generated—formal, or vertical, and informal, or horizontal, organizations.

The Five Kinds of Networks

There are many complicated and interesting theories about kinds of social networks. Most of the current theoretical work by sociologists seems to focus on abstract notions such as "weak links" and "hydra" networks.[1] For the practical network builder, however, the five networks model is an easy way to identify the persons with whom you exchange information.

Personal Networks

Your personal network consists of your family and friends. Your core personal network includes your parents, children, and immediate relatives, as well as any other relatives or friends who participated in your upbringing. These people constitute the touchstones of your life and they are the ones to whom you would be most likely to turn in times of crisis. Also included in your personal network are people you encounter outside of work, such as your dentist, the person who cashes your check at the bank, the supermarket checkout clerk, and the head of your child's day care center.

Schools are generators of personal networks. The feeling of a strongly knit school community is not unlike that of a family; indeed, the language of the hearth creeps into descriptions of relationships among various members of the school community. Some of the people in your personal network might not be individuals you would have chosen as a friend or relative, all things being equal. Nevertheless, you have a bond with them that either of you would find difficult to break.

Think about the last time you told one of these people about your work and how important it is to you, or the last time you asked a relative for help on a project. Judith Dome, a middle school teacher in an urban neighborhood, invited her mother in to conduct an after-school class on wardrobe and fashion for a group of preteen girls. She made a point of not telling the girls ahead of time who their "instructor" was. Her mother, Judith reports, did an excellent job, but the real payoff came when the girls realized that the nice woman with the expertise with color and scarves was their teacher's *mother!* It made a special connection for the class.

Tricia McCormick, another teacher, says one of her best teaching experiences was the time she and her mother taught together in a summer school program connected with an inner-city church. The program combined reading readiness with crafts and a smattering of religion. Watching her mother work with the children gave her a model for patience and understanding.

Geographic Networks

Neighborhood Networks

Relationships that grow out of living in proximity to someone are the most basic kind of network. These networks are built upon familiarity and common issues that affect people who live near one another. Depending on where you live, you might have a cordial, first-name relationship with the people in your immediate vicinity. Or, if you are like many urban dwellers, you can go years without knowing the names of the people in your apartment house. Nevertheless, people who identify themselves as having a connection to a particular geographical area have an automatic affinity with people who share that connection, whether it is to an apartment building, condominium complex, block, city, or nation.

What some people call official neighborhoods are usually bound together by political boundaries. These are the kinds of networks that meet at the polling places and official neighborhood organizations; these neighbors share concerns about police and fire protection, tax districts, crime watches, and property taxes. Property owners and business professionals are usually the most active participants; they typically are also the ones who feel the most strongly about a new bond issue or any other financial obligation imposed by the local school district.

Neighborhoods can also be defined by nonpolitical borders, such as terrain (e.g., mountain communities), ethnicity (e.g., "Little Italy" or "Chinatown"), proximity to a prominent landmark ("the university district"), or proximity to an event (the local "Great Flood"). For example, families living in a widespread ranching community located along the plains between Santa Fe, New Mexico, and Denver share strong bonds of friendship despite the miles that separate their homes. For this widely scattered "neighborhood," events such as high school basketball games turn into community dinners. One participant says that after each game, the home-team families eagerly wait for the visitors to leave. Pies and coffee magically appear, and the ranchers and their families stay for hours sharing companionship, news, and recent experiences.

Even experienced network builders tend to overlook the people who are part of their neighborhood networks, because they are so obvious. For example, few school employees would think to send open house invitations to the people who live across the street from the building or to introduce themselves to nearby business owners. All too often the only time a school becomes visible in the business community is when there is a problem, such as alleged shoplifting in a convenience store close to the school, or when there is an opportunity to make money, such as when students call on local merchants to sell ads in a school publication.

Making connections with the people who are part of your immediate geographical network need not be intrusive. The old-fashioned ways of building rapport with neighbors still work, from sharing an extra basket of fruit at the holiday season to stopping off to say hello to the new folks on the block. Even if your work precludes leisurely visits with the people down the road, you can still keep in touch with a note stuck in a mailbox and an appearance at a weekend garage sale.

Neighborhood networks are easy to tap into via voter registration lists and through events like special elections. You and your school can participate in a neighborhood network by collaborating in a crime watch program or developing an educational program on fire safety in the home that extends to all of the people in the physical neighborhood of the school.

The importance of neighborhood networks lies in their diversity. They usually include people with widely different occupations and values. Depending on your neighborhood, you might be able to make significant contacts with people in large corporations, government agencies, and funding organizations. You might also get valuable feedback from people outside your profession about the schools in your area.

Community Networks

An example of a community network is the community arts fair, such as the ones that grow up in urban neighborhoods near major inner-city universities like the University of Chicago and Columbia University in Manhattan. In small towns and rural areas, county and specialty fairs offer similar opportunities for people who identify with a particular place to come together.

Community networks are often generated by special events, which are easy to connect with through the planning office of the organization that oversees the events. Of course, the time to start building rapport with these people is well before the event, ideally in the downtime between periodic celebrations. It is in these slow times that you and the event planners can have enough time to develop mutually beneficial projects. Some complicated projects have a development clock that actually overlaps the events. For example, it is not uncommon for a large annual fair to have committees assigned anywhere from 18 months to 3 years before the particular fair for which they are responsible.

Larger Community Networks

For some people, community means any person or institution that lies within a self-defined area of influence. You might be pleasantly surprised at who considers your school or institution part of their personal territory. For example, you can network with your peers in schools and institutions in other parts of your state who might have similar problems. You can communicate positive facts about your school to your local, state, and national elected and appointed officials. You can make the local and state media aware of what your school is doing by including them when you send out press releases.

One way to get in touch with the larger community surrounding your school is to draw a map showing the school in the center of concentric circles radiating out to: (1) the borders of your state, (2) the edges of the natural boundaries of your region (e.g., Pacific Northwest, Maritime), and (3) the borders of the country. Identify three media sources serving each circle that you have not contacted in the last year.

Reclaiming the School-Community Relationship

For generations, schools have been rooted in the communities of their students and families, but urban busing programs, the consolidation of small rural school systems into huge, unified districts, and the transient nature of modern life have fragmented the traditional feeling of place associated with schools. Recently, however, a revival of school community building is beginning to reverse several decades of alienation. For example, feelings of neighborhood attachment are being exploited by community activists in inner-city neighborhoods where the socioeconomic status of the community has changed. Middle-class and wealthy alumni are being asked to contribute to the success of their former primary and secondary schools.

Some of the best efforts at nurturing the community-school relationship are taking place in Chicago and its suburbs. The Alliance for Achievement Network of the Academic Development Institute and Urban Traditions are two examples of outreach organizations with excellent print materials for teachers, parents, and community activists. Urban Traditions focuses on ethnic and cultural heritage issues, while the Alliance for Achievement Network is an organization for promoting the community school model as it is defined by shared values. Both have excellent publications. See Appendix C for more information on these organizations.

Personal Interest Networks

Some network theorists claim that shared interests are a requirement of a network.[2] Actually, the only requirement of a network, according to the definition used in this book, is the ability of the participants to exchange information. However, the most common network-building organizations are those where people have come together because of a common interest, whether it's growing rare roses, playing chamber music, discussing international politics, enjoying recreational bowling, or sharing professional news and ideas. Formal and informal interest networks can be important support groups for personal goals and desires such as career development and companionship.

Most educators belong to one or more professional groups. However, to build useful networks for your school it is important to remember that most people outside the school do not belong to school partnership organizations. Instead, you will find them through their formal and informal networks. Shared interest networks are a good place to start your search. The most successful network builders balance their connections between groups where they mingle with their professional colleagues and groups where they are the only educator.

Most people have many connections based on personal ideas and interests. Professional associations are one kind of shared interest network. Other kinds include study groups, clubs, sports teams, and networks formed through interests like birdwatching, stamp collecting, sewing, and investing in the stock market. Shared interest networks are generated around nearly every human activity, from oil painting to stock car racing, from a passion for science fiction to membership in the local art museum. People who share such interests seem to find each other, even without a formal organization. The local phone book, magazines that cater to special interests, the chamber of commerce, and national and state directories of trade and professional associations can help you identify some special interest networks. Here are examples that include both formal organizations and events that generate informal networks.

1. Clubs

2. Professional associations

3. Sports and recreation

4. Trade and business groups

5. Exhibitions, lectures, and conferences

6. Trade fairs

7. Sales and auctions

8. Movies

9. Stores and restaurants catering to special interests

10. University classes

11. Government agencies

12. Nonprofit organizations

13. Publishers, magazines, newspapers, and galleries

14. Parades, rallies, and picnics

15. Celebrity events

16. Fundraisers

Networks Based on Shared Values or World Views

Formal networks based on shared values are found most often in the context of religious organizations. Informally, these networks are composed of people who see "eye-to-eye" on subjects like educational reform, disciplinary policy, and the latest school bond issues. Values are a strong basis on which to build that special rapport that restores your own convictions about your life. Shared values create strong personal bonds. The weakness inherent in values networks is that the participants tend to be less diverse than in other networks and may be vulnerable to accusations of racism, sexism, or elitism.

Cultural, linguistic, historical, or religious ties are the glue that holds together most networks based on world view. They are emotionally powerful and can be useful in terms of relating information rapidly to large numbers of people. The most common cultural networks are based on place of origin—whether actual, ancestral, or one a person feels a strong affinity for. If you are fortunate enough to live and work in a multi-ethnic area, it is likely that you have a rich variety of cultural networks to contact.

Language is another network builder, even though most people regard a lack of skill in English to be a defect in this society. Instead of thinking of foreign language as a barrier, the successful networker can consider other languages as links with all kinds of interesting people. The key to building ties with other cultures and those who speak different languages is to meet them on their turf and with their language. Fortunately, there are many resources for the school staff member interested in establishing contacts and incorporating the wisdom of cultural networks in the classroom.

Acknowledging and Accepting Differences

From the outside looking in, the members of any group tend to look more similar than they are. Subtle cultural differences are ignored or dismissed as superficial. This can be a painful issue in dealing with cultural diversity, particularly in urban areas where it is likely that immigrants from the same parts of the world have settled. To the general public, Laotians seem the same as the Vietnamese, and people who speak Spanish, despite enormous differences in culture and places of origin, are all regarded as Hispanic or Latino.

The most successful network builders can acknowledge and accept someone else's viewpoint; this is very different from agreement. Building useful, long-term relationships that can survive battles over censorship, racism, sex education, dress codes, religious beliefs, and other issues that relate to the world views of parents, teachers, and school board members is a critical strategy. If in doubt, ask yourself whether you are building relationships that will survive after a particular battle is over. This means a rigorous adherence to gracious and civilized behavior and an avoidance of hasty words. It also means that every document that goes out from the school should focus on the positive goals of the school and avoid ad hominem attacks against any opposing groups or individuals.

Networks of Intent

Political organizations, unions, and activist groups of all kinds are the classic generators of networks of intent. Grassroots networks often start because of a perceived common danger. Short of a natural disaster, nothing can bring people together faster than the curtailing of what they consider a political or economic right.

Ironically, some school system administrators forget this basic characteristic of human nature when formulating and implementing plans. For example, an urban school district decided to bus several hundred high school students who had discipline problems into an abandoned school in a peaceful neighborhood. Even the local city councilman was left out of the discussions. Unfortunately, the administrators putting together the plan forgot to take into account such fundamental neighborhood issues as parking, land use requirements, and the plans the community had already made for the property. The resulting outcry was documented in several major newspaper articles. Within a week, dozens of citizens came forward to protest how the program was conceived, and several neighborhood organizations and the local community newspaper activated their supporters. An ad hoc committee is now monitoring the program.

As the above example shows, some networks of intent might also be called networks of intensity. Such networks can be created in a relatively short period of time by an event that is picked up by the media. They tend to have a hot "flashpoint," but little staying power. By contrast, people who are involved in a cause for the long haul tend to have a lower profile and ignore how topical a given issue might be.

The most common examples of networks of intent are political organizations, ranging from the block association that is working to get a stop light placed at a dangerous intersection to the upper echelons of a national political party. These kinds of networks are usually formal, with a hierarchy of leaders and bylaws that determine what the organization can do.

School network builders should approach political organizations with caution, because of regulations that forbid government employees from getting involved with politics or from spending government funds or paid time working on a political cause. However, you can make sure that your school projects are visible to the people in such organizations without running afoul of regulations. Appointed officials and government employees can be receptive to contacts from schools for information. A friendly contact within the bureaucracy can help you and your school find data necessary for decision making, warn you of upcoming legislation that might affect your professional life, and generally help you ease through government mazes. Network groups like FEW (Federally Employed Women) also can help.

Don't neglect to include in your network advocacy groups with whom you disagree. A proficient networker can maintain friendly but neutral relationships with all kinds of people in all kinds of organizations, short of vicious and violent hate organizations. For instance, Mabel Baker was a college media specialist concerned about the abortion issue. She used some mutual friends in the media to seek out her counterpart in the "other camp" and invited her to lunch. The two women found that they had more in common than they imagined and promised to keep in touch. Later, when Mabel's side was quoted in the press out of context, her contact was able to smooth the ruffled feathers in her own organization after Mabel had called to explain the error.

Serious network builders need to stay removed from the infighting that occurs in politically motivated networks. Although you may be passionate about some topics, you will benefit from learning the discipline, wisdom, and compassion needed to include your political opponents in your networking web. It cannot be emphasized enough that your best intentions for building useful relationships to support the goals of your organization can be thwarted by your own biases toward individuals of a particular philosophical or political bent.

Because networks of intent tend to build around causes and are short-lived, it is hard to keep track of them. Mapping them is especially important during times when you need the participation of the entire community to save a failing school or to raise money for a district.

Mapping Your Networks

When you consciously begin to build networks to support your work and the work of your school or institution, it is useful to begin by identifying your own personal network and focused networks. What networks do you already have? Where do they begin? Are they created by formal organizations or through informal connections? The number of people in your current networks is probably higher than you think; according to social scientists and advertising consultants, it could range from 250 to 1,250 or more! Remember, these are not necessarily your best friends and most congenial colleagues. They may include people you went to high school or college with, neighbors from a previous neighborhood, or co-workers from another job. It is true that the bonds of friendship and shared experiences might grow weaker after a few years, particularly if you neglect them. However, you probably know many more people than you think you do.

To map your own networks, read the above descriptions of the kinds of networks and participants that exist in the average person's life. Write down the names of people included in each of your networks. Then determine: (1) whether you have contacted these people about projects you are doing at your school, (2) whether they are up to date on your career and on the needs of your school, and (3) whether you are up to date about their lives.

Share this information about the kinds of personal and focused networks with colleagues and friends. (This is an excellent "brainstorming" exercise when trying to define new audiences for a project.) You might be surprised at how the maps of others' personal networks are different from your own. You might also be amazed at how much your maps overlap.

The staff of F.U.N.D. (Foundation for Urban and Neighborhood Development, now part of the SRM Corporation) in Denver has an excellent program for educating community network builders on how to identify formal (horizontal) and informal (vertical) networks. F.U.N.D. pioneered much of the work in identifying how people relate to each other and how networks define a community. See Appendix C for information on how to contact SRM.

Formal versus Informal Network Generators

What if you see a need for a particular kind of focused network? Should you call a meeting and set up some bylaws, or should you call individuals and bring them together casually as the need arises? There are advantages and disadvantages to both approaches.

Some networks are generated by formal organizations, such as professional associations and institutions including political parties and special interest clubs. Directories and educational magazines list hundreds of major national and international professional associations for education professionals, including such diverse groups as Agricultural Communicators in Education, the National Alliance of Black School Educators, the National Association of Educational Office Personnel, and the National Rural Education Association. Each of these presents opportunities for building connections with people who share particular education-related interests and concerns.

Other networks are created by informal association. A good example is a group of friends who meet and get to know each other because they ride the same bus to work every day or because their children attend the same school.

Formal Network Generators

People who build formal network generators tend to be those who feel comfortable with the structure of meetings, minutes, and newsletters. Consider some of the advantages and disadvantages of building a club for networking.

The advantages of a formal network generator include:

1. Easier to document to superiors
2. Easier to justify time spent
3. People like structure
4. Participants can be rewarded with prestige of office-holding
5. The formal structure can easily relate to other structured organizations
6. A "real" organization is easier to finance
7. The organization can survive past the founders
8. Easier to explain to people
9. Attracts people who like comradeship
10. People can be assigned formal roles

Some disadvantages of a formal network generator include:

1. Will tend to become a new bureaucracy
2. People who are not members may feel left out
3. Requires a regular time commitment for meetings
4. Easy to focus on things other than pure networking
5. Can be seen as competing with other groups for time and resources
6. Requires a lot of bookkeeping and paperwork
7. Creates a sense that networking can only happen at meetings
8. If disbanded, can create sense that networking doesn't work
9. Can require heavy investment of funds

Informal Network Generators

An informal network generator could be as simple as a bulletin board or a potluck supper. The artistry of creating just enough structure to hold people together is much like that of the grand party giver, who loves people and good conversation. One reason that so much has been written about formal generators is because informal generators are taken for granted; however, the informal network generator is actually much harder to create intentionally. Most seem to arise organically from situations.

An informal network generator has the following advantages:

1. Can be easily incorporated into more formal activities

2. Can adapt to many situations and kinds of organizations

3. No clear definition of members to create an elite

4. Inexpensive to operate

5. The only paperwork involved is keeping track of people and connections

6. No formal meetings to compete with other groups

7. Can focus on building relationships, not building a club

8. Portable and replicable

9. Attracts people who usually hate structure

10. More relaxed and conducive to fun

The disadvantages of an informal network generator include:

1. Difficult to justify to superiors

2. Difficult to document for funding

3. Hard to explain what you are doing

4. Can degenerate into a purely social hour or party

5. Sometimes lacks short-term results

6. Hard to formally interact with structured groups

7. Very fragile

8. Can easily be dominated by difficult people

9. Can turn off people who want something to happen

10. Rarely survives past the founders

Using Information about Networks

The best way to use the information in this chapter is as a tool to facilitate communication with other people. This might seem obvious, but many people who network professionally are painfully aware that the more time they spend analyzing theory, the less time they spend talking, writing, and listening. Some of the country's best network theorists are not necessarily the best network builders.

If you tend to get bogged down in discussions about what network a certain group has generated or the difference between networks of intent and networks of interest, it is time to slip out of the room and take a walk—to a local park where you will have the chance to chat at random with some people from the community.

Notes

1. See Appendix C under "Contemporary Information and Communication Theory" and "Professional and Personal Development" for books on network theories. The International Network for Social Network Analysis, headquartered at the University of South Florida, is considered the premier academic organization devoted to disseminating information about social network structure. See Appendix C for more information.

2. The Networking Institute is an organization that studies networks as organizations of like-minded people. See Appendix C for information.

---- **4** ----

Building Networks inside Your School

The first step in building trust and support within your own institution is to recognize and act on your power to influence the attitudes of others in a positive fashion. The ability of a single person to set the tone for an entire school is one of the most powerful tools a network builder has. If you are a principal or other school administrator, you have an especially strong influence, and you may be able to lay the foundation for better communication with only minimal changes in your behavior. Following are two examples of how school leaders were able to improve communication among staff members.

During a workshop, the executive director of a community school asked how she could improve the attitudes of her office staff. Every morning she had to walk through a "gauntlet" of desks to get to her office. At each desk sat a person with a serious, sad, or frowning face. She wanted students who came into the office to see happy people. "How can I make my people happy?" she asked ruefully.

"Let me guess," the facilitator said. "When you come in to the office in the morning, you are concerned about efficiency and productivity. You use the time while you walk to your office to ask questions about late reports and to check on the progress of various projects. Is that correct?" The director nodded.

"Your staff respects you, but I think they are a little nervous when they see you coming in the morning; they are accustomed to getting the third degree from you about work. Let me suggest a different approach. Next week, when you go in to work, make a point of saying hello to each staff member personally, without any mention of any work-related project. Smile at each person; act as if you are genuinely glad to see all of them."

"But I am," said the director.

"You have to prove it to your staff, not me," was the reply.

A week later the director called the facilitator. It had taken only a few days of her new, friendly behavior for the staff members to start smiling in the morning.

In another case, a group of public school teachers cited their principal's critical attitude toward them as their biggest complaint about her leadership style. The principal was willing to bring in an outside trainer to work with her and the teachers to improve the flow of information and ideas and to improve the level of trust. The simple fact that the principal spent the time and money to address the problem and was willing to participate in the workshop immediately raised the collective spirit of the teachers.

What if you are not the top person in your building? How much influence do you have? More than you think. An administrator who works on the management staff of a state board of education was faced with a problem of rapport building. Having come from the corporate world, she wore formal business attire to work, including tailored suits and attractive and expensive-looking jewelry. She saw herself as a "no-nonsense" type who did not indulge in gossip or visiting with other staff members during the day.

Although her professional accomplishments were beyond re-proach, the administrator began to receive poor evaluations from her supervisors. She knew she was alienating others in the office because her dress and demeanor set her apart from them. She decided she was not willing to change the way she dressed, but she was willing to change her behavior. She began spending five minutes each day conversing with each person on her manage-ment team. At first, people reacted with puzzlement and even a little hostility. Why was she being friendly all of a sudden? However, it took only a few days to win them over. Her next evaluations, in her words, did a "180-degree flip."

Start with the Basics

The first step in building a personal support network among your colleagues is to return to the same friendly and courteous behavior you demonstrated when you first became part of the school. In the same way that a marriage can go bad because spouses start taking each other for granted, professional relationships can sour when relationships among colleagues deteriorate into the kind of casual rudeness many people experience in their own families.

Like the community school director, you may be well respected, but your staff might be a little afraid of your criticisms. Like the principal, you might be well intentioned, but your staff thinks you don't support them enough. Like the board of education manager, you might be doing your job well, but your formal approach might be putting people off. In fact, if you are like most people, your perception of how well you are communicating and your colleagues' views of your efforts might be quite different. Good intentions in communications are not enough; the responses you receive are the measure of your success.

Mending Bridges

This means that any existing problems between you and other adults in the school need to be resolved. If you are serious about building networks in your school, now is the time to patch up old quarrels and set aside old grudges. Chances are, people you have clashed with in the past are as eager as you are to "let bygones be bygones."

A school librarian decided she was going to end a spite match between her and a teacher that had been going on for two years, ever since she had unintentionally insulted the teacher by asking him to lower his voice in the library. He had left in a huff, vowing never to return. When a note appeared in an academic journal about the publication of a paper he had written, she sent him a congratulatory letter. She claims he must have showed up in the library seconds after the note appeared on his desk through interdepartmental mail. He begged her pardon for his actions and promised to return to the library as a regular patron. The librarian was astonished at how easy it was to end the quarrel. What's more, she could not remember why she had waited two years to do something about it!

Not every personality conflict can be resolved this easily. Sometimes there are legitimate reasons to dislike someone or to disagree with her behavior. However, even someone you dislike can be a valuable part of your network. Ironically, the simple act of networking might be enough to end the dispute, although it may not happen overnight. It is difficult to resist someone who is being nice to you without either fawning on one hand or expecting an instant reward on the other hand. The innately friendly nature of most network transactions eventually can overcome many bad feelings.

Networking Fundamentals

1. Focus on the simple, common courtesies.

Saying please and thank you, using the other person's preferred style of address, and looking at people when you talk to them are basic communication skills. However, whenever people in a group complain about poor communication and low levels of trust, these "common" courtesies are often lacking.

2. Find sincere reasons to compliment people on something specific about their appearance or behavior.

It is appropriate to congratulate someone on an award or a personal triumph in the classroom. However, compliments should not be used as "lessons" commenting on past mistakes. "Wow, you lost a lot of weight over the holidays; I guess that heart attack scared you into changing your behavior," will not win friends in the teachers' lounge. Neither will, "I like your hair a lot better since you grew your bangs out," or, "I heard that you are going to school at night; does this mean you are planning to improve the way you run your math classes?"

Make complimenting the person your only goal; don't add any other issues. This can be difficult if you have a history of bad feelings with the other person. Recognizing that it will be difficult and practicing beforehand can make the conversation less awkward. In a network-building workshop, a school media specialist was trying to find something nice she could say about a certain teacher she openly detested. Every time she came up with something, she could not help but add a qualifier. Her first attempts, which she practiced while paired up with another school librarian, were unintentionally hilarious.

"Congratulations, I hear you won the bowling tournament. What a stupid hobby."

"I dislike the blouse you are wearing less than most of your wardrobe. You have really tacky taste."

During this exercise, the facilitator made sure the group

supported the media specialist with good-humored and gentle laughter; no one was allowed to make fun of her struggle. (Sarcasm and cruel putdowns have no part in any communication, but they were reported with disturbing frequency during interviews with teachers.) The facilitator and the group helped the media specialist understand that she needed to reconnect with her "enemy" and leave behind the need for revenge. She left the workshop clutching a piece of paper with several positive and usable examples.

Was this contrived? Yes, but only in the sense that the media specialist became aware of how her communication was affecting her peers and decided it was worth making an intentional effort to change her ways.

3.   Find out what is important to other people.

The first rule of network building is be useful to other people. Before you can build a working relationship with another person, you need to find out what he cares about and what he is doing about it.

A skillful network builder is a skillful interviewer, with the ability to draw people out. How much do you know about your colleagues? Who is devoted to their pets or is struggling with a home remodeling project? Who is trying to learn a new language, plan a trip to Mexico, or find a home for a stray puppy? Who is looking for a way to motivate a shy student to participate in a drama class or needs ideas on an art project for a substitute teacher? These clues can lead you to all kinds of nice connections on behalf of other people.

The hardest part of building school networks is the tendency for people in helping professions to want to be self-reliant and to refuse any kind of assistance. Some of your fellow school staff members might think that your attempts to help are actually subtle putdowns or a way of showing off. Others may be ungracious or defensive. These behaviors are useful indications that you might have misread the best way to approach people.

4.   Ask other people for help.

The best way to show educational professionals how to build networks is to be willing to ask for help first. If you have a reputation for being the one with the answers, the exchange of information among your friends and professional acquaintances will tend to be one-sided; distributing advice and solving other people's problems without letting them reciprocate is not network building. By showing that you are willing to ask for assistance, you provide living evidence that network building is based on reciprocity and a respect for everyone's contributions.

The new head research librarian of a large university media center used asking her staff members for help as a way to break down communication barriers. She had been hired away from another university to take over the department, where some of the librarians were a generation younger and slightly in awe of her national reputation. She overcame their shyness by purposely asking them for help on reference questions in front of patrons and by openly showing both respect for their knowledge and gratitude for their assistance.

Networking throughout the Institution

As in any organization, members of a school community tend to group themselves according to job description and level of education. Individuals identify closely with job titles, credentials, and experience; a "sixth-grade reading teacher with a master's degree and 15 years of experience" is presumably at a higher level than a "second-grade teacher with no advanced degrees and 6 years of experience." "Higher level" can translate into "better" in some people's minds.

Network builders don't have time for such artificial hierarchies. Teachers are responsible for modeling appropriate behavior for students; this includes treating every fellow staff member with respect and courtesy. Students are more aware than you might think of conflicts between teachers or other staff members; they can feel the tension. Elaborate, well-publicized partnership programs are meaningless if they are not backed by mutual cooperation and respect.

Some network builders acknowledge the difficulty of building working relationships in institutions by differentiating between "networking up" and "networking down," based on the commonly held perceptions of the participants. It is best to start by building rapport with those people who are "above" you in the structure. It is important to realize, however, that building networks does not replace the legal and political structure of the institution. As Robert K. Mueller points out in *Corporate Networking: Building Channels for Information and Influence* (New York: Free

Press, 1986), networks do not and should not replace the infra-structures of an organization. However, networks do seem to flourish where the structures have become oppressive.

The purpose of network building inside an institution is:

1. To improve the flow of communication in all directions

2. To further every individual's ability to serve herself, her community, and her institution

3. To build trust and rapport

Be careful that your zeal in tearing down barriers does not accidentally destroy a crucial load-bearing wall.

The Administration: Networking Up

There are three secrets to building networks with supervisors:[1]

1. Treat them like fellow human beings.

Remember that human beings are imperfect. Human beings have crises at home, bad days, headaches, ambivalence about their jobs, and the prerogative to change their minds without notice. Human beings may get tired and cranky but feel the need to pretend nothing is wrong. Human beings often fail to practice what they preach. The same is true of principals, superintendents, and members of the school board.

Use the same courtesy, respect, and kindness toward your supervisors that you use with anyone else in your networks. Assume that your principal is likely to be dealing with the same kinds of issues that you and your peers encounter, from overwork to concerns about job security to frustration at the ineffectiveness of the school system. Don't neglect to invite the principal to participate in network-building events, from speaking at the school career fair (she can describe her experiences as a principal) to signing up for the babysitting co-op.

2. Assume they feel isolated.

The great paradox about leadership is that being at the top often removes people from the information they need to do their jobs, just when they need it the most. There may be real or imagined psychological barriers between the administrator and the rank and file. It is common to hear teachers complain that decisions affecting the classroom are being made by people who have never set foot in a school or listened to the concerns of teachers, parents, and students. But top people often have a harder time reaching out than those whose jobs are lower on the rungs, so it is frequently up to subordinates to make the first move.

The secret is effective communication. Tirades and anonymous memos are not useful, but succinct, neutrally worded memos with specific information are. And, just as when working to build rapport with peers, sincere compliments can do much to open lines of communication.

3.   Offer solutions that take their point of view into account.

Next time you have a terrific idea for your school, put yourself in your principal's shoes and ask what extra headaches the idea may create for her before making your proposal. Individuals who have strong empathy for each other's points of view are able to offer each other assistance based on the real limits of their jobs. Even if you don't agree with your principal's opinions and ways of operating the school, you can go further in negotiating change and improving trust if you assume she is doing the best she can at the moment. If you acknowledge her concerns and fears, many of them may vanish, because you have removed the need for her to defend her position.

Teachers and the Professional Staff: Networking Across

If you are a teacher, school media specialist, special education teacher, social worker, or other trained professional on the staff of a typical school, you may be painfully aware of where you are in the pecking order. Perhaps you have been the target of gossip or have participated in ostracizing a teacher yourself. How can you change the situation?

1.   Start with a buddy.

Find one person, preferably someone who is "different" from you in some specific way and whose networks are significantly different from yours, with whom you can begin to design strategies. You might begin by agreeing to support each other in swearing off negative gossip about co-workers or in spreading good words about someone who is getting picked on. Your buddy might be the one you call for emotional support in times of high stress. You both agree to help each other, and anyone else in the school, when things get tough. Perhaps she can walk with you at lunchtime when you are trying to lose weight, or you can give her crucial feedback when she fails to win support for a new idea.

The idea is not to build a new clique or power base. Instead, you are developing a new attitude in the school, one that demonstrates the flexibility and open mind of the good communicator. To do that, you need to have friends who are far enough removed from your position to give you a sense of perspective. This might mean finding someone from a different grade level or someone whose job is different.

2.   Be patient with yourself and your colleagues.

It took years to build up whatever system of noncommunication exists in your building; a few weeks of good intentions is not going to create instant trust. Prepare to be surprised at how willing some people are to participate immediately, while others remain firmly entrenched behind walls of distrust.

3.   Actively seek out diverse contacts.

Acquaint yourself with the people who are doing a job different from your own. At a school picnic, spend time talking with staff members whom you don't get to see during the course of a school day. Ask the school social worker, the nurse, and the counselor about their jobs. Remind yourself that you can learn from everyone in your school.

Professional Support Staff: Networking Down

It is important to treat every adult in the institution as your colleague. Some teachers have an unfortunate habit of talking to other adults the same way they talk to children in a classroom. This can cause support personnel to feel as if the teachers and other professionals are being condescending. Sometimes such teachers have little experience relating outside the work environment to staff members who are of a different ethnic or racial background or who live in a different part of the community. Language can also be a barrier if members of the support staff are recent immigrants from another country, but it is not useful to assume automatically that communication problems are rooted in racism or sexism.

In some schools, students feel more comfortable relating to support staff, who may share their socioeconomic background, than they do to the professional staff. One student tells how her time at an exclusive boarding school was made easier by her unofficial adoption by the family of the groundskeeper. Their raucous family dinners were more like those at her own home. Don't be surprised if the custodian of your school knows more about the home lives of some of the children than the school counselor does.

The old Dale Carnegie approach of being interested in other people and what they do is the best way to break down barriers. Start with a friendly hello, and, as with all interactions with adults you do not know well, use a formal address unless they ask you to do otherwise. The practice of addressing elderly cafeteria workers by their first names, while they are expected to return the salutation with a "Yes, sir, Mr. Jones" does not exemplify network building at its best.

Rapport building also occurs when different categories of employees are encouraged to talk with each other about what is important to them. A secretary at a small religious college felt isolated from the rest of the staff because of personal problems. Although she was a competent employee, no one had been able to break through her icy reserve. She was amazed at the support she received when she shared her burdens in a workshop on network building. She was certain that difficulties she was having with an alienated married daughter were unusual; she was shocked when a show of hands revealed that several other clerical staff and teachers had experienced the same thing. She told the group that just knowing that other people had lived through the same sorrows would make it easier for her to come to work.

Consultants, Substitutes, and Traveling Teachers

Individuals whose presence in the school is temporary or fleeting often are overlooked. Some regular staff members resent the interruptions and envy the perceived freedom of those who seem to come and go at will. However, these individuals have a special value in your network-building efforts.

1.   They can be ambassadors for your school in the larger community.

The substitute teacher who chooses to "sub" rather than have a fulltime job often has more opportunities to interact with other adults, outside the field of education, during the normal work day. She can distribute brochures about school functions and present the school's mission and goals in the course of conversations with people throughout the community.

The ways that temporary personnel are treated by your permanent staff determine what is said about your school. A freelance performer who specializes in music and theater programs in elementary schools says he can tell within minutes of arriving at a school how the school is run and how students and teachers are treated. In some schools, everyone he meets is immediately interested in who he is and what they can do to help. An adult rushing through the halls will stop to smile and say hello and ask if he needs assistance. The place where he is to perform is ready for his final touches, and someone has even remembered to get him a cup of coffee and a donut. On the other hand, he has gone into some schools where his presence was treated with indifference and even downright hostility by staff. In one case, he even had to convince a disbelieving secretary that he had indeed been invited by her school to come to perform that day.

2.   They can be made to feel a part of the school.

For some traveling teachers, the difference between a good and bad experience in a school is whether they have a little corner to call their own. It might be as simple as a drawer in a file cabinet with a lock or a special place to hang their hat. For others, it is being included in decision making in the schools, from receiving announcements and newsletters to being invited to attend meetings and inservice trainings. Even if they are unable to participate, the effort goes a long way toward helping substitute teachers feel that they are part of your school community.

3.   They have a sense of perspective about the students, the physical plant, the curricula, and staff performance that the regular staff might lack.

The occasional visitor will notice such things as a slow deterioration of the attitude of staff toward welcoming strangers or a change in the quality of meals in the school cafeteria. This perspective can be used to improve the quality of the school, if school staff members choose not to be defensive.

Including Everyone in the Process

In his workshops to improve the performance and morale of an entire school district, trainer Peter J. McLaughlin started with the bus drivers. He figured that they were the first school personnel the children encountered every day and that the attitude of the drivers could influence the attitude of the students and, thereby, change the feel of the entire school day for everyone. One measure of his success is that complaints against the bus drivers have almost disappeared. Another measure is that the drivers themselves have come to realize that they do more than drive the bus. Not only are they responsible for the safety of the children, but they are also the gatekeepers for the institution.

A network builder values each and every person in the school and considers each person a partner in the process of improving the shared school community. An award-winning teacher, known for her exceptional communication skills with both staff and students, kept herself going through difficult days with a simple secret: "As I rushed through the halls of the school between classes, I only knew the names of about one-third of the students and not all of the teachers and staff. But with everyone I passed, I said a brief prayer for their well-being. It helped me remember the value of each person."

Students as Networkers

The subject was career connections, and the sessions were packed to the rafters. The assignment was simple. Each participant was asked to stand up and describe her career goal. She was to give any information she thought would be useful to the rest of the group about what she was trying to accomplish. The audience then was asked to respond with advice in the form of contacts with possible employers or mentors.

In one session, a self-possessed blonde stood up and announced her desire to become a professional concert pianist; she needed connections with people already in the field. The first audience member who stood up invited her over for dinner; the conductor of the local symphony was a friend of the family, and the audience member was willing to orchestrate a meeting. The rest of the audience burst into enthusiastic applause.

Most of the sessions were like that. Participants had requests for information about new careers in space and science, teaching, and research. No matter how unusual the request, it seemed that someone had information about a special class or program or personally knew someone in the field.

There is nothing especially unusual about this kind of networking, except that it happened at a Girl Scout conference and the audience participants were mostly junior high school students. The girls knew the hobbies of their teachers, the occupations of their parents' friends and neighbors, the occupations of their friends' parents, and the interests of friends at church and in community groups. Many of the girls were sophisticated about their information and had advice on how to approach the proposed connections. One shy and scholarly looking girl became quite animated when discussing her love of computers and her willingness to invite a stranger from the workshop to accompany her to her next users' group meeting.

Even quite young children can participate in networking. A seven-year-old girl wanted to use a networking and information service just as her mother did, but she wanted to have her own account. When asked how she would pay for her account, she suggested that she could get her school to sign up for the firm's services and that she could promote the business at the school's career fair. The agreement was struck, and the firm had a new paying client.

What Can Students Offer?

1. Valuable feedback about the success of school programs from their point of view

The founding editor of a national magazine for high school newspapers says that it still surprises her how often school reforms are planned with no input from the students. The failure of many great ideas in education, she says, can be directly attributed to keeping students out of the evaluation process. In an article in *Preventing School Failure* (Summer 1990), Mary T. Peters makes a strong case for including students in evaluation meetings with parents and teachers. The article, "Someone's Missing: The Student as Overlooked Participant in the IEP Process," sets reasonable guidelines for making sure students understand what is expected of them in such a meeting and are respected as part of the education team.

The danger with student participation is that adults tend to pick the students they like or who fit the stereotype of "good" students. These students are not necessarily the natural leaders or representative of the views of the majority of their peers.[2] One principal maintains that the best student programs in governance and collaboration involve every student, even if it means rotating duties indiscriminately through the entire student body. When a group of students chosen to lead student activities turned out to be the ones with the biggest problems inside and outside the classroom, many teachers were skeptical. The students decided to put on an all-grades party that turned out to be the hit of the school year. The kids on the committee, reported the principal, were walking 10 feet high the rest of the year. Programs like this teach students that responsibility toward one's community is not synonymous with winning elections, being popular, or being part of the "in" crowd.

2.   Connections by means of their own personal networks

A college librarian, working on her first book, shared the good news with her students and asked them for help. Some of her best leads came from the students, she says.

Children of all ages are great network builders, both for themselves and for the adults who care for and about them. Most love to volunteer; the trick is to value every contribution and make every contributor feel appreciated. Be sensitive to the fact that children might not feel that their contributions are welcomed because of economic or cultural differences. An intern at a business was shy about offering anything at a workshop on network building, until the facilitator coaxed out the fact that her father was a well-known restaurateur whose barbecue sauce was legendary. Instantly, she became the center of an envious circle of executives and was recruited to help plan the next several company events. The adults marveled that she knew how to plan a picnic for several hundred people. Skills that she took for granted (hadn't she been working in her father's business since she could walk?) were viewed as valuable by the adults.

3.   Support for school policies

Students can influence adults outside of the school system with their attitudes about school policies. One study of student attitudes toward teachers and schools shows that children will support efforts that are "tough" if they are perceived to be "fair." According to Denver-based trainer Peter J. McLaughlin, the students he surveys say that teachers must have a sense of humor to be effective and that a tough teacher who is fair is not disliked.

4. Involvement in school activities that help the school and the community

Many teachers say that they want their students doing some kind of community service as a way of reconnecting them in a positive way with the adult world. The rewards to the community are enormous, as students learn to wage battles against pollution, crime, and corrupt government in their community.

A budding young investigative reporter in a midwestern high school was able to uncover discrepancies in school budget reports and was credited with the inexplicable restoration of budget funds to the school district's art and music departments. Other students are working in nursing homes, restoring wildlife preserves, monitoring city council meetings, planting gardens, running businesses, and writing letters to the editor.

There is nothing new about any of these activities, except that many school officials are giving such programs a new legitimacy. The key is for adults to treat students with respect and reward their efforts by taking their concerns seriously. One of the strongest principles of educational and developmental reform, espoused by Maria Montessori, George Dennison, John Holt, and others, is that school and childhood are not preparations for life. They *are* life, and too often adults dehumanize and degrade children by not respecting their concerns at an early age.

Notes

1. It would be helpful to learn what professional networks that serve the profession say about the challenges of being a principal. Two such organizations are the National Association of Secondary School Principals, 1904 Association Drive, Reston, VA 22091, (703) 860-0200, and the American Association of School Administrators, 1801 N. Moore Street, Arlington, VA 22209, (703) 528-0700.
2. Gary Bergreen's *Coping with Difficult Teachers* (New York: Rosen Publishing Group, 1988) provides insights into how students are affected by stereotyping on the part of their teachers.

5

Building Networks outside Your School

"Teachers are the only professionals who spend the whole day in a room without their own phone."

Lisa Carlson of Metasystems Design Group, Inc., headquartered in Arlington, Virginia, is an internationally known expert at creating communication systems for schools and other institutions. In making the above comment, she pointed out that the most basic and prevalent "networking" tool in our society is unavailable to most teachers during working hours. Except at the university level, few teachers have the luxury of an office with their own extension number. Few schools provide their teachers with business cards, personal stationery, or a budget for joining civic organizations or going to conferences outside their field. How can teachers, media specialists, and other school personnel build working relationships outside their institutions without the networking tools and budgets accorded other professionals?

Time is also a problem. Few teachers can leave a school building during the noon hour to attend community meetings; monitoring lunch hour and attending conferences and meetings inside the school are part of most teachers' regular duties. The example of one school professional and working mother is not atypical. The wife of a rural superintendent of schools, she may accompany her husband to four sports events in one evening, all of which are being held at different schools in a far-flung farming and ranching community. She herself is a school librarian in another district, and, of course, she and her husband try to be supportive of their

61

own three children, who go to school in two different towns. Such necessities as a new pair of glasses to replace the pair she lost and music lessons for her talented children are a two-hour drive away in the closest city.

The irony of school employees who, while demanding more involvement on the part of their students' parents, are struggling to juggle their own parental responsibilities and demanding jobs, is not lost on teachers and administrators. An elementary school teacher with three sons admits that she is not the responsive parent that her children's teachers expect her to be; also, she does not live up to the demands she has made of her students' families in the past.

Keys to Networking Success

Despite these obstacles, many teachers and school community members are building successful networks. There are several keys to their success:

1. Motivation

People who make time to build networks outside of their school do so because they believe that investing in the community is of the highest importance. Those who do not believe that this is worth their time and resources usually make excuses for why it cannot be done and reserve their energy for other efforts. Ironically, one of the best reasons for network building is that it can help solve personal stress issues for educators, by giving them a community of supportive people to rely on.

The principal of a grade school in a small town uses part of his limited budget to print business cards for teachers and support staff. He does this because much of the success of his school depends on volunteers in the professional community. Part of each teacher's job is to sell the importance of the school to the community. The payoff has been enormous—the teachers have helped recruit dozens of volunteer instructors for noontime enrichment programs. The principal also believes that the business cards are a relatively inexpensive morale booster for the teachers and staff. An assistant staff member in the library "lit up" when she got her own school business cards. Her supervisor wanted her to believe that she was making a real contribution to the school, and the business cards convinced her it was true.

2. Eagerness to expand your point of view

As Lisa Carlson points out, teachers "do their business behind closed doors." Consequently, like many busy professionals, they and other school personnel tend to associate mostly with others of their profession. This, coupled with the amount of time they spend with children and young adults, makes some educators feel awkward dealing with business owners, scientists, university professors, librarians, factory workers, and other adults in the community. School personnel must believe in themselves as real professionals with a contribution to make to the larger community.

Building connections with other adults does not have to be limited to dry business meetings. A busy first-grade teacher says she makes time to do creative things outside of her classroom such as participating in dance classes, both as a teacher and as a student. It keeps her energy level high during the week and allows her to make useful connections for her students and colleagues. Otherwise, she would feel isolated in the classroom with few opportunities to interact with other adults.

Teachers who are excited by their work as teachers are usually strong network builders. They have strong ties with the community through a connection with a church, hobby, community cause, or youth organization, or they previously pursued other careers besides education. Their contacts that were conducive to building supportive relationships were the ones that made a difference, not just friendly and superficial social contacts. "My outside activities keep me sane" is a sentiment echoed by many teachers and school personnel.

3. Eliminating less useful activities and replacing them with activities that further your goals

Every successful professional is forced to make decisions about how to spend time. It might seem that every demand on your time is one that is impossible to change. Communication consultant Jan Prince suggests examining each demand with two questions: (1) What would happen if I changed what I was doing, and (2) how do I know this is true?

The program director of a community education project was looking to advance her career. A divorced mother with two teenage children, she wanted to return to school to complete a master's degree but could not see where she could make the time. When pressed, she said she did not want to take evening classes because she did not want her teenage children to be left alone two evenings a week.

What would happen if she did go to class? The director did not think her children would wreck the house or starve to death. But she did have a sinking feeling that they would think she was a bad mother if she was not there as cook, chauffeur, and confidante every night of the week.

How did she know this was true? She was guessing, she admitted. When she asked them how they felt, her children were enthusiastic about her plans to go to school; the grumbling about losing their private driver and chef for a couple of nights a week was minimal.

Teachers with busy schedules do not necessarily see themselves as better time managers than their colleagues with fewer outside activities and friendships. The truth seems to be that "you do what you want to do." But what about the demands made upon school personnel that seemingly cannot be compromised? Paperwork is always a problem, especially for those whose programs come under the direct scrutiny of state and federal agencies. Missing a deadline could mean lost funding or, in a worst case scenario, fines against the school system for noncompliance. Or what about the requirements of the state board of education or local school district or the mandates of the principal? How do successful network builders find the time to handle these?

Successful network builders at all levels of the school system report that, in many cases, people who follow every rule and regulation do not perform their jobs as well as those who know when to let what things slide. The overly conscientious teacher, for example, never learns to differentiate between meaningful structure and bureaucratic busy-work. One important characteristic of a leader is the ability to know when to ignore the "little" things. Much of the paperwork school personnel take on qualifies as "little stuff." How can you know? Ask experienced colleagues what are the ramifications of a particular action and test your premises. During network-building workshops, it is common for a teacher to say that he cannot do something constructive because of an ironclad rule. Someone else, however, will report that she has successfully been navigating around the same rule for years.

Getting Started

Recruiting supporters for school projects or beginning the process of creating more formal partnerships is something that can be done in as little as five or ten minutes a day. Start with phone calls or letters to get a feel for the kinds of programs or opportunities other people are considering; you might find that many people in your community are interested in helping the schools.

The biggest obstacle for many would-be networkers is their assumption that particular people and organizations would not be interested in exchanging information and ideas with them. This is rooted in the premise that teachers and other school professionals come to the larger community only to beg for money and that no other transactions are possible. A frequently used exercise in career planning books suggests that readers learn to evaluate their life experiences in terms of the skills they have learned. Teachers and school personnel can practice the same technique and learn to appreciate how much they have to offer other professionals, including patience, organizational skills, and conflict resolution skills.

Here are some examples of categories of people that you can include in your network building. Under each heading is a list of ways to start networking with that particular group of people. Also included is a list of "needs" and "wants" with specific examples drawn from interviews, workshop exercises, and the experiences of school personnel as reported in professional journals and magazines about school-community relations. Use these examples to start your own network-building activities.

Parents and Families as Resources

A successful elementary school teacher who makes it a point to have home visits with each student's family says that she makes sure the first visit is always informal and unstructured. Her job during the first meeting is to let the parents know who she is and what interests her as a person; at the same time, she finds out about the lives and interests of her students' parents and siblings. This can lead to discoveries about shared values and interests, from a common love of pets and gardening to home towns, political party affiliations, and mutual friends.

Connecting with Parents and Families

1. Start early.

The first day of school or before, send the parents a positive communication, such as a flyer or postcard, welcoming them as partners in their children's education. Make it brief and friendly, and make it a personal communication from you to the parents, not from an institutional professional to a faceless adult.

2.   Contact parents personally.

As soon as possible, begin contacting each parent or guardian with a brief hello, either over the phone or in person.

Pretend that family members are your "customers" and find out a little about them in a neutral, nonintrusive way. It is not necessary or desirable to ask highly personal questions. If the parents believe you are genuinely interested in them as people, they will usually open up, if you are able to be quiet and listen.

If you begin calls and visits early in the school year, you will be able to contact almost all of the parents or guardians before the end of the winter holidays. Then, if a problem should arise, you will have already had one positive contact with the parents on which to form a basis for discussion.

3.   Make all of your communication respectful.

Some professionals call the adults they serve by their first name while expecting a formal address in return. Start with a formal salutation, whether in writing or in person, and let the other person decide if the conversation should be less formal. You can suggest that the parent or guardian call you by your first name, and let them tell you if they want a less formal address. You might think this is an obvious courtesy, but too many parents complain about how they are treated by school personnel; "Manners 101" can't be overlooked.

4.   Make all of your communication appropriate.

"Appropriate" means appropriate to the culture and customs of each family. A social worker who works with teenage drug and gang issues in publicly funded housing projects was at first taken aback by the generosity of the poor families she serves. They literally would offer her the last food in the house if she stopped over for a visit. If she turned it down out of concern for their finances, they would feel insulted. She quickly learned that being a responsible and gracious host was more important to these families than the risk of going hungry.

To cope with these kinds of potential misunderstandings, at least one Texas school district has issued a brochure on religious customs, so that school personnel understand the nuances of dress, beliefs, diet, and other behavior of non-Christian students and families. Other districts around the country provide cross-cultural training, videos, and brochures to assist school personnel in understanding other cultures. It is not just immigrant and poverty-level families who need this special understanding. The wise network builder does not assume that all people in the immediate neighborhood are the same and is aware of and respects even subtle cultural differences.

5. Be consistently above reproach in all communications with all segments of the community.

At an all-day school-business partnership program for aspiring young scientists, the keynote speaker was dismayed at the behavior of the school personnel and the staff of the partnership group sponsoring the program. A few teachers made racist comments to each other and to the speaker, who quickly expressed her displeasure. When the students arrived, accompanied by adult relatives, the teachers overtly ignored the parents, uncles, etc., but went out of their way to greet the officials and the business leaders who attended. No visible attempt was made to make the parents feel comfortable or welcome. However, the organizers made a big fuss over the dignitaries.

The literature of this school-business partnership organization was impressive, with many of the largest corporations in the state listed on the masthead. The program was held up as an example of successful school-community relations. Talks with community leaders revealed that at least two other significant organizations in the community had experienced identical problems. Not surprisingly, the partnership organization failed to continue to garner enough financial support from business and folded a few months later.

A happier episode involved an elementary school receptionist who treated everyone who walked into her office with a cheerful and helpful attitude. During one hectic morning, she skillfully assisted a new immigrant family with passable English through filling out a maze of school forms. Throughout the process she answered the phone several times with a friendly voice and warm manner despite the confusion in her office, and had time to give a helpless visitor in jeans and a worn coat directions to the library. She treated everyone with enthusiasm and seemed sincerely glad to see them. During the short time the immigrant family was in the office, the receptionist noted and remembered the names of every family member. As she talked, she used their names repeatedly, always with the correct pronunciation. The parents beamed as she walked them to the door of the office and expressed her pleasure at their enrolling their children in the school.

Every parent and adult in every school community, in every setting, should receive the same courteous treatment.

What You Can Do for Parents

1.   Communicate frequently with good news about their children.

Use brief notes, phone calls, or personal visits, depending on what is most likely to reach each parent.

A junior high school teacher insists her home visits provide priceless information. It was through a home visit that she discovered that the mysterious change in behavior in a formerly well-behaved and friendly student stemmed from the teacher's remarkable resemblance to the student's single father's new girlfriend, a fact that might not have come up during a parent conference.

2.   Ask for feedback about your performance.

An elementary school teacher admits that she might not have had the self-confidence to ask parents for their opinions and ideas when she first began teaching. Now, however, she says she has the maturity to be able to listen and learn from others, without feeling overwhelmed by criticism.

3.   Ask questions about their perceptions of the school and their children's activities.

4.   Offer resources to deal with challenges such as homework, discipline, crime, drugs, peer pressure, health, etc.

You can develop your own favorite list of books on parenting, drugs, nutrition, and other family issues to share with parents. (All of these books should be available at your school or public library.) Also, you can see yourself as a partner with parents in locating the answers to all kinds of questions. The following list illustrates some of the needs many families face:

- Emergency housing, food, and clothing services
- Information on good children's health services

- Places to find directories for summer camps, day care, family-oriented activities, resorts and vacations, and toys, books, and games
- Information on job programs for teenagers
- Information about scholarship funds
- Contacts with private schools and programs for students with special talents, in addition to the usual listing for "gifted and talented"
- Information related to the elderly
- Services and social programs for single parents

You could keep a list of phone numbers of possible contacts for dealing with these and other problems, culled from local directories and from conversations with other good network builders. In many cases, the names of a few public agencies or clearinghouses can supply most of the answers a family needs; coordinate your resources with the school social worker and counselor.

Remember, you don't have to know everything about everything. All you need to know is a likely place to start the search for information. You can distribute the burden of managing the contacts among other members of the school community. Everyone can share the same central list of general contacts, but it is likely that one person has the most up-to-date information about coping with food stamp programs, while another teacher has the best contacts with after-school programs for junior high school students.

5. Listen.

Many professionals think they have to solve everyone's problems. Sometimes the biggest service you can offer to parents is to listen, with sympathy but without comment.

6. Ask for their help in specific ways.

Open-ended and vague requests for assistance can frighten away the most determined volunteer. If you tell a parent, particularly one who does not have a history of volunteering, about a small project with a beginning, a middle, and an end, you are more likely to get a positive response.

7. Praise them for their good intentions and hard work.

What Parents Can Do for You

1. Be an active partner in the education of their children

2. Provide you with support, inside and outside the classroom

3. Offer you a perspective about their community and networks

4. Offer assistance inside and outside the classroom

5. Provide resources: people, projects, and ideas

6. Bring to the school community sets of skills, credentials, and education that are different from those of the teaching staff

Neighborhood and Community Resources

Much attention in the educational world is focused on formal organizations for teacher-parent cooperation. Good networking can support these efforts. However, if you work in a building or district without any effective formal structures, you can build powerful networks without any need for meetings or special funding.

In many urban, suburban, and rural neighborhoods, the school building is not in proximity to the people it serves. The businesses, homes, farms, and industries in the immediate neighborhood may be strangers to that big brick building with all of the noisy kids. Yet people in the immediate neighborhood can be a wonderful source of information and support, if they are given the opportunity.

Connecting with the Neighborhood

1. Identify the members of the immediate community.

Who lives and works in the neighborhood? Who are the local elected officials? Who owns property? What are the main concerns of local property owners? (These are taxpayers who pay a substantial portion of your budget out of their property taxes!) What are the economic concerns of the business owners and workers? Which are the significant community organizations, such as the churches, community centers, senior centers, and charitable and cultural organizations? Who heads the law enforcement agencies? Which people are perceived as the community leaders? What other institutions are offering educational services in the immediate vicinity of your school?

Obtain or draw a map of your school neighborhood. This information is invaluable for identifying resources and creating coalitions and alliances. Mapping a neighborhood also can make an interesting sociological study for classes. For example, how many elderly people live within a four-block radius of your school? How long have they lived there? What do they think of this generation of children? Local genealogical societies can provide information about how to conduct oral history interviews.

2.   Communicate regularly with your neighborhood.

A private elementary school that moved into an abandoned church in a close-knit neighborhood was greeted by an angry homeowner threatening a lawsuit. He was an artist who was sure that the clamor from the schoolyard at recess would destroy the peace and quiet of his studio. School staff, however, had gone from door to door weeks before they made the move and had built their network of support with the community through conversations with dozens of people. The lone homeowner found this out when he tried to have the school removed and discovered that none of his neighbors would sign the petition or participate in the threatened lawsuit. The staff of the school was able to placate the man, and they continued to be good neighbors for the six years they were in the community. Many residents of the neighborhood were genuinely sad to see the school go when it moved to larger quarters several blocks away.

Ask your neighborhood newspaper to start a section on school news and announcements aimed at school families and the larger community. At the same time, you can have your school newspaper or student literary magazine distributed door-to-door by students accompanied by parents or school personnel.

3.   Treat your neighbors as part of the school community, even if they do not have children.

Use the "network with everyone" guideline to communicate with seniors, singles, childless families, small businesses, agencies, and churches. Draw a "sphere of influence" around your school and use your information about your school's geographical network as a guide to the diversity of people you influence and serve.

4.   Invite your neighbors in.

It might not be obvious who your neighbors are if your school building is a large new suburban school built in the middle of nowhere, nor might it be obvious why they would want to come to visit the school. Start by assuming that everyone in a certain geographical region is a neighbor and that everyone appreciates an invitation. How about highway workers, gas station attendants, agricultural station researchers, real estate office staff, and airport personnel? This is a good time to practice your creativity. For example, schools often can head off problems with local religious leaders over misunderstandings concerning the difference between teaching "religion" and teaching the influence of religious thought in history, literature, etc., by inviting the participation of those leaders in councils, workshops, and other activities.

What You Can Do for the Community

1.   Provide facilities for community activities

2.   Offer expertise in planning and education for other educational projects

3.   Offer the involvement of students in projects to help the community

4.   Cooperate in community issues such as crime control, neighborhood beautification, and traffic management

5.   Support local charities

6.   Provide links with the local library system

7.   Provide a physical focal point for communication in the neighborhood

What the Community Can Do for You

1.   Provide a supportive atmosphere for citizenship and learning

A business owner in one inner-city neighborhood has developed a working relationship with the local junior high school concerning the behavior of students in his large parking lot near the school. School rules dictate that students who misbehave within a four-block radius of the school are subject to school discipline. For a brief time, students tested those rules on his property with shoving contests, short fights, and loud obscenities shouted at passersby. The business owner called the school and learned from teachers how to give students some appropriate reminders of the school rules. Within a week, the incidents had stopped.

2. Provide resources to stretch your budget

3. Offer ways to honor students and other members of the school community for their achievements

4. Help to attract families and staff to the community with good jobs, low crime rates, reasonable tax rates, and cultural amenities

5. Enrich students' lives with information about careers, opportunities, and different aspects of the world outside their school

6. Provide opportunities to broaden the perspective of teachers and other school personnel

7. Reinforce the positive values of the community

The Media as a Resource

Faxed press releases, videotaped "brochures," and a professional public relations staff do not guarantee supportive media coverage. Many of the media people interviewed for this book reiterated that media relations start with person-to-person communications. Getting these connections in place is much more important than writing snappy press releases.

Connecting with the Media

The Written Link

1. Learn how each particular media outlet wants their information and give it to them that way.

This comes as a pleasant surprise to some people who think that there is only one standard "way" to communicate with the media and that if they don't know "the way" they will be ostracized or embarrassed. Even experienced reporters and editors must learn new methods of doing things when they move from one radio station, newspaper, or television station to another. How do you find out how a particular station or publication wants to receive information? Call or visit them and ask. Media professionals are glad to help members of the community learn what is needed for a press release, public service announcement, or news conference.

Remember to call the media organization directly rather than rely on second-hand information. Make yourself and your school institution personally known to the magazine, newspaper, and broadcast station personnel in your area.

2.   Understand deadlines.

Although the image of news coverage in this country is based on the spectacular achievements of reporters rushing to the scene of a crime or disaster with live reports, most reporting is planned days and weeks in advance. The cover story for a Sunday magazine supplement in a major daily newspaper might be shot and written two months before it is published. On the other hand, the coverage of the Iraq–United States conflict caused the media to throw out hundreds of planned features, columns, and local news stories for weeks after the beginning of the war.

A good rule of thumb is always to discuss coverage with your media contacts as soon as you know approximately when an event will be held, even if it is weeks away and the date is not yet firm. Let them tell you when to request coverage. Many reporters will offer valuable advice about getting the word out about your event. In larger cities, print and broadcast outlets even offer classes on dealing with media and publicizing events.

3.   Don't overload them with faxes.

For all of their glamour, facsimile transmissions are useful only for the fast-breaking news needs of the electronic media in larger media markets. Rolls of fax printouts can pile up on the floor next to a fax machine even during a slow newsday at a radio or television station; the producers know that most of the transmissions come from politicians, government agencies, and public relations "flacks" who could have just as well sent the information, which is rarely urgent, by mail.

Faxes are useful when there is an emergency and you need to send detailed, specific information the same day. A "snow" day;

a report on a school fire, a tornado, or an unexpected school shutdown; or a school district response to accusations of misconduct are cases when the speed and accuracy of the fax machine is needed. (Remember to "blow up" your fax transmissions by 10–20 percent to ensure legibility at the other end.)

4. Take the time to write to the right person.

The most tedious task of network building with the media is coping with the "revolving door" found at many newspapers, radio stations, and magazines. One radio station contacted for this book had two general managers, three news directors, four program directors, and three major format changes in a twelve-month period, during which five different people were in charge of public service announcements!

Always ask the receptionist for the name of the person who should receive your information; then, continue to use the receptionist as your key contact. The receptionist can always tell you who is the latest "right" person; he or she can also confirm that you have the correct titles, pronunciations, and spellings—important information if you want to avoid giving offense the first time you open your mouth.

5. Submit perfect copy.

Typos and spelling and grammatical errors reflect badly on your own and the school's professionalism.

6. Involve students.

Students can write press releases and develop copy for school features. Your local media representatives will be pleased and impressed to see students, even those in the primary grades, taking an active part in communications.

7. Develop exchanges of talent and information.

Most school newspapers develop exchange programs with other schools to swap papers and ideas. How about doing the same with your local papers? Ask an editor to critique a paper with student writers. Have students write to newspapers and magazines and request a trade of publications. Newspaper and radio or television station internships are a great way to involve your students with the local media. Find out what is available.

The Spoken Link

1.   Provide a school phone directory.

Provide media representatives with a printed directory of school personnel's phone numbers and positions. Many school districts provide the name and number of a media specialist; this is not sufficient for the media's purposes. Most media people construct personal files of community leaders to contact during a crisis or while researching a story; make it as easy as possible for them to contact people in your school building or district. This can make the difference in the amount of positive coverage your school receives. This media directory also should list "secret" numbers for use in case of an emergency.

2.   Learn to make the "precision" call.

One gripe of busy news professionals is callers who, in an effort to be polite, waste time by not coming to the point. You don't have to be rude, but learning to give information succinctly will mark you as knowledgeable in the ways of the newsroom. For example: "This is Pat Wagner, the librarian at Lincoln School. We just received a national award for our reading program from the Ford Foundation. Would you be interested in more information?" Notice that the "hi, how are you" routine is eliminated.

The Personal Link

1.   Have a school/media open house.

Create special events at your school for the media to attend for information, not just to write about or broadcast. Invite them to come for fun events, for tours of the school facility, and for meetings to exchange ideas with school officials.

2.   Go see them on their turf.

The importance of showing up in person cannot be overemphasized. You will learn a tremendous amount about how your school can improve its coverage. Also, many of the most important people you deal with, such as assignment editors and the receptionist, will rarely have the opportunity to come to the school. Communications between your school and the media organization will improve when both sides have faces and personalities to connect with the disembodied voices on the phone.

3.   Use food as a lure.

Media professionals are similar to educators in that they do their jobs because they love them, not because most of them make a lot of money. Little perks often are all they get. The school that puts out the coffee and tea and offers fresh fruit or bakery goods during a media visit will be fondly remembered. A class project that culminates in a delicious meal is a surefire draw for reporters, particularly if you remember to make enough for a few adult appetites.

All of the rules of good network building apply to the media, including generous thank-yous. How about a box of homemade cookies to your favorite editor? It is absolutely shameless behavior, and it works!

When Things Go Wrong

Problems with dealing with the media can range from misspelled names to garbled discussions of complex issues to overt hostility from an editorial page writer. What can you do?

1.   Always maintain your composure.

Yelling and name-calling are inappropriate, as are sarcastic remarks and whining, especially when you might eventually want to talk to this particular person again or to request a favor from him. A common complaint among media personnel is the abusive attitude of community representatives who think the media have a legal obligation to publish or broadcast any and all information on worthy causes for free, regardless of limitations of space or time.

2.   Always express thanks for coverage and for the reporter taking the time to do a story or editorial, even if the piece is negative.

You can always thank them sincerely for their interest and concerns about education, without being sarcastic. You also can take the time to say thanks for favorable or fair-handed coverage of a school issue even if your school was not mentioned. Send the note or make the call directly to the writer of the story, and include some relevant materials from your own school. Compliments are so rare in the newsroom that you might get coverage for your next project without asking for it—one editor of a national magazine says she has received one thank-you letter in ten years.

3. Send in corrections, and thank the source when those corrections are published.

Almost all media outlets are conscientious about printing or announcing corrections. Be matter-of-fact about the correction, and don't assume hostile intent on their part.

Occasionally reporters and editors cross the fine line between objective reporting and editorializing. Your reaction to such violations of journalistic ethics probably will depend on how the article treats your school; few people complain about a favorable bias toward their own programs. However, in opinion pieces, editorials, columns, features, and letters to the editor, writers are expressing their personal opinions and ideas; you cannot demand that the paper print a retraction or correction of someone's interpretation of the facts.

Other Institutions as Resources

Network building with public and private institutions, such as businesses, libraries, government agencies, and schools, offers several special problems. First, institutions often are treated as though they are sentient and monolithic entities. Instead of talking about "how does Ed, who runs the local floral business, feel about our school," people tend to focus on "American Floral's attitude." People within institutions tend to talk about themselves the same way. The result is that it is hard to get a handle on whether the contacts you make are "official" or "unofficial" and whether those contacts carry the legal and financial support of the institution.

Second, individuals in institutions are not always good about taking responsibility for their own actions. "It is not my fault" is a sentence heard in large institutions of all kinds; it is particularly annoying when you discover that no one will claim responsibility for or the ability to do anything about your particular situation.

Finally, the byzantine maze of overlapping and misidentified territories within any large institution can frustrate the most sincere attempts on both sides to communicate. An informal survey of trainers and business owners revealed that customer service issues were easily the most important challenge for business in the coming decades. Businesses are responding to this problem of "customer service" at all levels; most public agencies are just beginning to change their ways.

Connecting with Other Institutions

Most books on community-school relations focus almost exclusively on "official" network building between organizations. But network builders must deal with two simultaneous "faces" to be successful in approaching institutions: the official and formalized public "face" and the informal and human private "face." In the beginning, the sometimes conflicting needs of each approach need to be balanced. Even small organizations can operate as formally as large institutions. With every kind of official group, from community chess clubs to the largest federal agency, you can benefit from using both approaches.

The Formal Institutional Network Approach

1.   Research the organization.

Use the library and your own friendly contacts to find out about the organization. Is it publicly or privately funded? What can it do officially for your school, if anything? What is its history of working with other schools and community organizations? Does it have any political alignments that might prove embarrassing to your school? Does it have a previous history with your school; if so, is that history positive?

What is the organization's reputation within its own networks? Is it considered effective? Does it have a history of collaboration? What groups has it helped in the past? Has there been a recent change in administration, mission, staffing, or financing?

If possible, obtain some of the organization's current literature, and visit the office or site before you begin the formal network building. All of this research can take time (if you have some well-placed network contacts, it might take just a few phone calls), but it can save considerable grief.

2.   Start at the top.

In all but the largest organizations, the top person will appreciate a letter, preferably from your top person. Some organizations have special departments assigned to deal with connections with the schools. These are usually identified as community relations, public relations, community partnerships, marketing, or public affairs departments or as the corporate foundation. Nevertheless, you might receive special attention if you let the top person know about you.

Ideally, your top person and their top person already know each other through common, influential networks. In fact, a few discreet phone calls with shared acquaintances might pave the way for a lunch to discuss possible joint projects. Even if the letter is funneled through the appropriate channels, its referral from the president or director's office will help give your request some status.

3.   Determine who in each organization will be responsible for your school and the institution keeping in touch.

Make sure both persons know that communicating with each other is part of their job and define how much responsibility each has for decision making. How will other interested parties in the school or the institution be kept apprised of what is happening? How will information and the results of collaborations be documented and publicized?

4.   Identify the responsibilities and benefits for both parties.

If a large corporation wants to help your school build a science lab and expects a certain amount of publicity in return, have them spell out exactly what they mean by publicity, with criteria for measuring results. If your school and the local library are conducting a joint literacy challenge to encourage parents to read to their children at home, identify the contributions in funding and staffing that each group will make. By spelling out deadlines and accountability before things begin, you smooth the way for future projects.

The Informal Institutional Network Approach

1.   Identify the connections your school already has within the target organization.

Several parents might work there or deal with the company on a regular basis. Some of your fellow teachers might have gone to school with members of the board. Use those contacts to find out more about how your school and the corporation might be of benefit to each other.

2.   Look for allies within the organization.

Count on the fact that in many organizations the right hand and the left hand are not playing a duet. No matter how good your official connection is, it will be uncommon for the rest of the company to know what is happening, even if the news of the collaboration is published in the company newsletter. Although you don't want to undermine the "official" efforts, you cannot afford to assume that everyone in the organization who would want to be useful to you knows who you are and what you are doing.

3. Build networks at all levels.

Any professional salesperson will tell you that the most important network builders in any institution are the receptionists and secretaries. The best have tremendous discretionary powers. Be sure that you personally thank the support staff of the institution for any assistance you "officially" receive.

What You Can Offer Institutions

1. Free or cost-effective publicity for their organization

2. A market for their services and products

3. A way to invest in the community

4. Specific information and expertise in educational issues

5. Connections with community and educational institutions

6. Partnerships in coping with community issues such as drug abuse

7. Input into the education and training of future workers

8. In secondary schools, a source of parttime employees

9. In some cases, information on tax breaks and credits

10. Support for their employees' families and children

11. Improving the attractiveness of the community to talented workers

What Institutions Can Offer You

1. Professional advice in management and finance

2. Contributions of money, staff, and goods

3. Opportunities for sharing physical assets, such as buildings and computers

4. Opportunities for student apprenticeships and internships

5. Mentors for "at-risk" students and those with special needs

6. Information about training programs and continuing education

7. Loans of equipment and technicians

8. Support during school bond elections and other public issues

9. Feedback about your effectiveness with special interest groups

10. Help in planning events with other organizations

Remembering Your Least Likely Allies

The local columnist who is critical of your new math program might be an enthusiastic supporter of the library. A business owner who will not sign a petition to get the county to increase funding for sports may dig into her own pocket to provide money for a scholarship fund. One outspoken economist who vigorously opposed a property tax increase for his district was very willing to speak to classes about the importance of staying in school. These positions are not contradictions. Just because an individual is opposed to one thing your school is doing, it does not follow that they will reject everything.

Here are a few of the kinds of people and projects that teachers and other school personnel have referred to as the "enemy," either in print or in conversations about network building at workshops. Do you regard these individuals or groups as your opponents or as potential resources for your networks?

1. Principals

2. School board members

3. Community activists

4. Parents

5. Heads of large corporations

6. Small-business owners

7. Newspaper columnists

8. Republicans

9. Socialists

10. Feminists

11. Religious leaders

12. Anyone who opposes a school bond election

13. Employees and supporters of private schools

14. Home schoolers

15. Employees of the federal Department of Education

Network builders are cheerfully stubborn. For the sake of their schools, they will talk to anyone, be friendly to anyone, and assume that some kind of mutually useful link can be made with virtually any group or organization. Rather than agreeing with the purveyors of "ain't it awful" and "aren't they terrible," the network builder sets out to prove them wrong.

Such reforms as school-business partnerships, community-school activities, accountability councils, and direct parental involvement will be a major part of the restructuring of the school systems in the coming decades. As time goes on, network building will prove too valuable a tool to ignore.[1]

Note

1. Current books on school reform, such as *We Can Rescue the Schools: The Cure for Chicago's Public School Crisis* (Chicago: URF Education Foundation, 1988); *Making the Best of Schools: A Handbook for Parents, Teachers, and Policymakers* (New Haven, CT: Yale University Press, 1990); and *Improving Schools from Within: Teachers, Parents, and Principals Can Make the Difference* (San Francisco: Jossey-Bass, 1990), all mention the importance of network building.

---––– 6 ---–––

The Network Station

The Ideal Station

A network station is a physical location in your school where information is exchanged. It has a file cabinet, telephones, a place to sit, a place to post notes, and a blackboard covered with urgent messages and time-critical information. A shelf or two hold directories and reference books, but most of the information is in organized disarray on large bulletin boards and in labeled baskets. The posted papers and notes include the usual collegial bulletins and journals, announcements of summer institutes, and brochures about teaching vacations, but the bulk of the information is generated by individuals inside the school building.

The network station is accessible to students, faculty, support staff, parents, and the greater community, and thus differs from the teachers' lounge or private work areas, which are seen as a retreat away from the demands of students and the outside world. Teachers who enjoy a little hustle and bustle around them while they are preparing lesson plans or grading papers might choose the network station as a place to do paperwork, but for most staff members it serves mainly as a place to converse and do research.

The permanent staff of the network station rotates among members of every sector of the school community: parents, student helpers, teachers, custodians—even the principal and the superintendent do a stint now and then. The staff's job is to answer questions and point people to possible resource persons or projects. Most importantly, the staff are good listeners.

This is where everyone in the school building comes for information about what other staff and students are doing in their personal and professional lives. Most of the information is practical. Who wants to sell their car or couch or tractor? Who is looking for a trusty tax accountant or family lawyer or dermatologist? Who is interested in taking advantage of the bounty from a summer garden of squash and tomatoes? Who wants to share a subscription to a professional journal?

Some of the exchanges are about ideas. Who wants to develop a student/staff book review newsletter? Who would like to discuss a new math tutorial that was touted at the last state teachers' convention? Would anyone like to develop an exercise program for students and staff during lunch periods? What are the pros and cons of the latest book on school reform?

The network station is also a place for people outside of the school building to communicate with the immediate school community. What students are selling what raffle tickets for what charity events? Which scholars or professionals are volunteering to come to speak to classes about their specialties? What local businesses are offering incentives for students to maintain good grades? What employees from local businesses have offered to tutor students in math, science, or history?

The network station is where the school baby-sitting co-op is coordinated among students, families, and employees and where people can find a list of local businesses that give discounts to school district employees. The network station phone number is the one the switchboard operator is most likely to give to a stranger calling in for information, and school visitors are directed here when they check in with the office. The community relations officer has a desk here, and when members of the school board or representatives from the superintendent's office come to visit, the network station is where they hang their hats.

Because the station is a fun place to be and adds so much to the quality of the lives of the people in the school community, it is a favorite place to hang out. Staffing is rarely a problem. Overhead is low, because information, for the most part, is "filed" in plain view and is time dated; it is a fairly rapid process to post new information and toss dated information into a holding bin for a month, until it is finally thrown away.

The only permanent file is a simple computer database that holds names, phone numbers, and addresses; each name entered in the computer has a few notes of information and perhaps five or ten keywords. The system is easy enough for the average computer-illiterate adult to run; the important programming and maintenance is done by students. Several Rolodexes are filled with frequently used numbers and names. Station staffers spend some time on the phone during each shift, calling people from the computer database and the Rolodexes to update information and stay in touch.

The network station acts as a rumor control office in stressful times and as a brainstorming center when the school staff and students are involved in major projects. The feelings of trust, mutual aid, and community it helps generate permeate the entire school building. In fact, the interesting contradiction of the network station is that the better it performs its services to the community, the less it is needed. The threads it weaves create more and more network building among a greater number of people. However, because there always are new students, staff, and families in the community and new challenges to face, the network station is constantly renewed.

The network station is a vortex of information, ideas, and people. It is where connections are made, and its presence supports the activities of many people and projects, without usurping their work. No one feels threatened by its presence; the staff is powerless to make policy decisions. Their only function is to build support networks.

The network station is an important and inexpensive key to helping schools survive the storms of reform. And yet, it does not really exist in almost any school or educational institution.

The Real Network Station: Does It Exist?

Many schools have people who are natural network builders. Regardless of their job descriptions or training, they are the most likely people to know what is going on and, in an unofficial capacity, to make the contacts. But these people rarely have time to devote to building networks, nor do they have the official authority necessary to do the job well.

Even if they are given official sanction to make contacts among members of the school community, network builders rarely receive time and funding for more than one school year, due to budget cutbacks, lack of official commitment, or politics. When the "unofficial" network builder for one middle school was finally made "official" (with, she reports, an entire 45 minutes each week to devote to the cause), her position lasted one year. Several failed school bond issues caused major budget cuts in her school; after the reshuffling was over, her 45 minutes a week was gone, and so was her embryonic station.

You might protest that the bulletin board in the teacher's lounge or in the student commons fills the need for a network station in your school. In fact, you might even think there are too many notes tacked up in odd places advertising used furniture and a need for donations to the pep club. A typical school has several bulletin boards filled with information for the professionals in the school, including colorful posters and notices about teaching fellowships. There are the usual well-done photo boards in the halls and classrooms, supporting the accomplishments of various classes, and an impressive display of newspaper stories featuring students, parents, and teachers.

All of this is important information, but the crucial person-to-person links are lacking. Nowhere is there a piece of paper that contains information directed from one human being to another. Experience has shown that bulletin boards and internal publicity about clubs and pep rallies are inadequate without the kind of personal contact that comes from people taking the time to communicate directly with other people.

The School Media Center as a Network Station

Many school media specialists have the training and desire to locate the school's network station in the media center or library, which may be the most logical place for it. Many librarians, however, still equate network building with archive building. The professional literature encourages school media specialists to "sell" their resources to their colleagues as a way of raising the position of the school library, and the school librarian, in the eyes of teachers and support staff. But the resources cited are almost always documents and computer software; rarely are person-to-person connections emphasized.

In workshops with school media specialists and other professional librarians, participants admit that they usually think of information in terms of physical collections, rather than as a process of directing a patron or student to a person or project. Further, many school media specialists are overwhelmed by short staffing, a lack of funds, and a lack of space. And too many schools lack libraries altogether and are forced to rely on local public libraries to provide all of their students' research needs.

Despite these obstacles, the personality of each school media specialist and the things that "turn her on" about her job are the deciding factors in how the library is run. This, in turn, determines whether the library will evolve into a network station. Some school media specialists are "catalogers." These are the archivists, whom some of their colleagues label as "traditional librarians." Some school media specialists are administrators and have their best relationships with other school administrators; they spend much of their time filling out budget forms and meeting with those in the school community whom they perceive as their peers. And some librarians are "tekkies" who focus on the most advanced computer equipment and audiovisual materials as the answer to their school's information management problems.

A growing number of media specialists, however, are "people persons" at heart. They are active marketing specialists who see books and computers as only part of what they have to offer to students and the school institution. They are the community-school advocates, who want the school libraries open after hours to adult learners and who shock some traditionalists by having the library host loud and messy events, from ice cream–making demonstrations to baroque concerts. Through their efforts, more and more school media centers are fulfilling the promise of the complete information center. Still, even a school media center with terrific community appeal will not automatically become a networking center. The key is in how the activities and personnel support the exchange of information and the working relationships among all patrons, including both students and adults.

How To Build a Network Station

If you feel that your school is ready for a more formal approach to building support networks, where do you start?

1. Start with the behavior, not the structure.

Network building must always begin with the behavior of individuals, not with the imposition of a new structure. Demonstrate your intentions and the benefits of network building, don't just talk about it. Being useful to members of your school community can begin with the kind of mutual aid found in a small town. Babysitting co-ops, information about rides, offers of free furniture and homemade candy, job opportunities for students, items for sale, and information about individual interests among teachers and staff are just the start. Show your colleagues that exchanging these kinds of information can help relieve the stress many people feel in coping with the demands of their personal and professional lives.

2. Identify the natural network stations and the existing network builders and support what they are already doing.

There are probably certain physical locations in your school that tend to attract people. The teachers' lounge is one natural gathering place, as are the mail distribution center, the locker areas, the teachers' end of the cafeteria, and the lobby of the administrative offices. In one midwestern high school, the journalism offices of the school newspaper and yearbook became a place where both students and faculty hung out, mainly to order photographs from the student photographers. It was a great place to pick up gossip and to leave press releases from service groups and special school events.

The personality of a particular staff person, as mentioned before, also can create a network station. Perhaps your business office has become a place for teachers to sneak away for a few minutes of peace, because of the filled candy dish and the sunny disposition of the secretary. Schools blessed with a tolerant and talented cafeteria staff might have a special corner of the kitchen or home-ec lab where there is always a fresh plate of cookies and a teacher or staff person can sit and read the paper for five minutes at lunch.

Your new idea does not have to replace whatever is already happening in your school; ideally it should strengthen existing efforts. Compliment the coach on his network building, and point out how his office is a valuable place to pick up information. Tell your colleagues how much useful advice you pick up from the bulletin board of flyers in the school counselor's office. Thank the secretary who puts out a spread of crackers and cheese on Friday for a lunch TGIF party and offer to chip in.

The worst mistake is to disrupt what is already going on in an organic and useful way with your efficient, structured, and controlled network office. However, you may see opportunities to increase the visibility and usefulness of the network building that is already occurring. Just make sure that your efforts will please and benefit the current participants rather than undermining them, by consulting with them before you take action.

3.   Sell the idea to the "powers that be."

If you are lucky enough to have a principal who believes in the usefulness of cooperative efforts, it will not be hard to convince him of the value of a network station. Or you might have the kind of laissez-faire administrator who wants you to take the initiative and tell her about it later. But what if you must sell this radical idea in order to receive the space, time, and resources to do it well?

First, enlist support from your existing network. If you don't have an informal school network yet, or if you are the only one who thinks this is a good idea, wait until you have a number of key members of the school community committed to seeing it happen. Then present your case to your administrator, emphasizing ways the network station will address his or her problems. If budget money is tight, don't say that you will need extra funds to make it happen. Instead, show how the station will save money by increasing the school's ability to tap into business donations. If staff is limited, show how the station will help deal with absentee issues by improving the "safety nets" of staff with family problems, such as finding day care for children or help with an elderly relative. And, if space is a problem, show how the network station will make a corner of the school that is inadequate for classrooms or storage into a productive space.

Support your case with documents and reliable sources that promote networks, partnerships, and other collaborative approaches to school management. Use the references mentioned in this book as a starting place to show how a network station, rather than disrupting the status quo, will strengthen the need for community involvement and better communication among staff members.

Keeping It a Success

You have the support of the school, your principal says yes, and you are able to use the empty cubicle in the office that everyone hates because it has no windows. How do you ensure that the network station is a continuing success?

1. Enlist the support of many people in the school to keep it running.

If you are not able to find different people to participate, it is better to close the station down than to make it your special project. In no time, you will have created a nice information office, but it will have lost the participatory flavor and the active involvement of the school community members it was designed to serve.

2. Keep new information flowing into it all the time.

Change the posters once a week, and be ruthless about throwing out dated or stale information on a regular basis. Your network participants should feel that every visit uncovers something new.

3. Keep it friendly.

Use bright colors on the walls. Greet every person with the attitude that you are happy to see them (as well you should be!).

4. Try to be useful to everyone by pointing the way, but restrain yourself from competing with the existing professionals in the school.

You might be a terrific listener, but be wary of trying to be the school guidance counselor or therapist, unless it is an acknowledged and accepted part of your job description.

5. Document and report your successes.

School libraries use circulation statistics to justify their growth (or existence, is some cases). You can't compete with "12,345 volumes loaned out during the month of December," but you can report how the station staff was able to track down $10,000 worth of free computers for the science lab and recruit several new parents to volunteer as math tutors. Tout your successes, and then use them to expand your networks even further.

7

Networking Tools

Most people who study network building think about the tools of the trade first: filing cabinets, libraries, computer databases, directories, and record-keeping systems. Ironically, the major reason network-building and network-generating organizations fail is because of an overreliance on structures, such as formal organizations, and on tools, such as computers and newsletters, rather than on the working relationships among individuals. Putting the majority of your time into constructing records of data is the "archive" approach; the ensuing overhead burns out the network builder and kills the organization.

Some record keeping is inevitable, if for no other reason than the fact that few people can memorize detailed information about hundreds, if not thousands, of people and institutions. However, the special requirements of a network database collection system are not taught in library school; even experienced and well-trained school media specialists can inadvertently create leviathans that overwhelm rather than create tools to facilitate communication.

The Dangers of Building a Network Archive

The easy part of networking building is locating the information. The hard part is cataloging, storing, and updating the information. If you are a school media specialist or librarian, you know how much time you spend filing and refiling documents of all kinds. In fact, at networking workshops held for school and public librarians, the most frequently mentioned professional item on the list of "needs" is "help me find time to file and read."

When clerical work is used to provide a mental health break from an overloaded day, it is easy to justify a massive filing system for networking contacts, on the principle that you are doing "good." It is easy to confuse *doing* good and *feeling* good. By all means, give yourself the satisfaction of organizing files and sorting brochures, but ask yourself how much of the information you are going to use once it is tucked into your neatly labeled and cross-indexed files.

Building an archive can take time away from the phone calls, postcards, and face-to-face meetings that are the heart of building working relationships with other people. Of course, the process of communication leads to the accumulation of all kinds of fascinating and important print documents. But for some would-be network builders, coping with a pile of newsletters and brochures is preferable to coping with human beings. After all, the pile of unread journals, magazines, and newspaper clippings on your desk might threaten to engulf you physically, but it doesn't ask annoying questions or cause you to stay up all night worrying about the last conversation you had with it.

The Ideal Network Filing System

The librarian who ran the filing system for a nonprofit, citywide adult education system reports that her daily success was measured by the number of student and teacher information cards she was able to create and file. The student body was growing rapidly, and often she fell behind. She had no time to spend answering questions or making contacts for students. She wanted to build working relationships among the students and teachers, but she had become a file clerk, despite her education and credentials.

The size of the filing system, representing the number of potential teachers and students, became the yardstick of success for the entire organization. The director urged the staff to recruit more and more students, but the librarian felt alienated from the process. Somehow, just logging in numbers was not enough for her. She left the school with the sense that building a network was about acquiring filing cabinets filled with cross-referenced cards.

When the school failed, she wondered if it was partly because of the amount of overhead incurred by the wall of filing cabinets; had the director lost sight of his original objective?

Following are some guidelines for a useful record-keeping system for the serious network builder. Some of the guidelines contradict expert advice in records management and librarianship. Many experts, however, are terrific at building archives and not so good at building relationships with information sources. "Information scouting" and other network-building activities are mentioned in their books, but only in passing.

Keep It Simple

This advice applies to everything connected with network building, from the entries in your address book, to the design of the community bulletin board, to the layout of the network newsletter, to the way information is exchanged among participants. You want others to be able to understand your systems without having an advanced degree in library science. The systems you devise should serve the participants, not hamper their ability to communicate with each other.

Though nice to have, a computer is not an essential networking tool. One skilled and successful school psychologist still operates her network out of one file box, filled to overflowing with the names of specialists in education, medicine, mental health, women's issues, and the law. Even large networks can use simple methods. The 15 formal networks of an international religious education organization with thousands of members use postcards as their primary method of communication.

Keep It Inexpensive

No matter how much funding you receive at the beginning of your network-building project, and no matter how successful you think you will be at attracting grants, fees, and paying members, cost control should be a key factor in designing your record-keeping and communication systems. Spend your money on the important things.

It makes sense to buy a power conditioner for your computer system; the extra $20 to protect your equipment from a "surge" or "spike" can save thousands of dollars worth of hardware, software, and data. It makes sense to have your primary materials translated into the languages of your community. It makes sense to spend a little extra for healthy and good-tasting refreshments for a meeting. It does not make sense to print a newsletter on expensive paper or to use a full sheet of paper in an envelope to mail a memo when a postcard will do. It does not make sense to have a four-color logo professionally designed for your organization just to impress potential funders. And there is no need to buy a full-color map of your city from a map store when your local newspaper, chamber of commerce, or county commissioner's office might be able to give you one, albeit printed in black-and-white, for free.

Buying expensive items can put a great deal of financial stress on both formal and informal networks. In a private study of information services produced by a Ph.D. candidate from Cornell University, all but one of the groups polled said money was their biggest problem. The one that did not also was unique in that its staff used the computer system less than any other group did. Most of the groups mentioned in that study have vanished in the intervening years, except for the one with the modest overhead.

The trappings of a formal network organization can force the staff to spend more time fundraising and less time making connections. It also perpetuates the "waiting for the grant" syndrome that infects many individuals trying to build bridges between school personnel and the rest of the community. Network building is not about budgets; it is about sharing ideas, an activity that can be done from a card table in a supermarket as well as from a lush office in a penthouse.

By focusing on money you may miss opportunities to seek donations from the community, which help build a shared sense of involvement and ownership. Money can become a barrier for people who want to help but who think that the personnel of the network organization care about them only for their cash contributions. It may be better to do without the formal tools until the relationships among the participants are strengthened.

Finally, focusing on expensive facilities and tools is a good way to hasten the hardening of the bureaucratic arteries of even a small organization. It is a morale booster to have up-to-date equipment and a nice place from which to operate, but treating yourself and your organization to the latest in computer equipment and expensive file systems carries a hidden price. More time and energy may be spent on "organizational" issues rather than on communicating with people. Even the most idealistic and radical of school-community organizers can fall prey to the contagion of building a monument to their own importance.

Keep It Flexible

This applies to both computer programs and file card systems. Ask a science librarian how many times the U.S. Patent Office in Washington, D.C., must revise its categories to cope with new discoveries. Ask the manager of the classified section of a newspaper how many times new products, such as computers, time-share condominiums, Vietnamese pot-bellied pigs, and facsimile machines, require the addition of new categories.

The hubris of system designers is a tendency to think that it is possible to anticipate all the future requirements of an information system. Instead, heed the advice of the school computer consultant who told his class to always include a category for "other," even in the simplest of file systems, to take care of the unexpected.

If you do have your heart set on a computer system, find out what happens when you change your mind about how you want information organized. Some databases are set in concrete; others are flexible. It is rumored that system designers for a West Coast magazine, when setting up categories for their online computer system, decided to use the alphabet. A letter was assigned to each of 26 categories. This system worked perfectly until the participants began to come up with ideas that fell outside of the fixed categories. It seemed that the programmer of the system had assigned only one letter space to accommodate the code for each category.

One approach is to start with no categories and allow the responses of network participants to dictate how the information will be organized. Most information in a network system or publication tends to organize itself to suit the individuals involved. It is important to understand that different groups of people will have different ways of looking at and using the same information. A network of school board members, for example, might search for information about children differently than a network of teachers, a network of parents, and a network of students. A community center with a network of before- and after-school care providers might find it more useful to catalog information according to zip code or neighborhood, rather than by category of day care facility, if that is the way most of the requests for information are defined.

Sensitivity to the way information is categorized in a diverse community might mean that you end up with more than one cataloging system. In some situations, information about minorities will be cataloged separately; in others, the information will dovetail into general categories. Which is preferable? Perhaps both, if it can be managed. Flexibility is important, because people organize and select information differently based on their own priorities and prejudices. The interactions of people do not fit neatly into the Dewey Decimal system, nor are they confined to the ordered disciplines one might find in a college catalog, where interdisciplinary collaborations are still the exception.

Keep It Portable

An individual network builder is often on the move, spending as much time as possible on other people's turf. Therefore, the core network information, which consists of names and contact information for the participants, should be in some form that is easy to transport. "Portable" does not mean a briefcase filled to overflowing with papers, index cards, and manuals. A simple phone list would make a better start.

What Works

In the beginning, a well-annotated address book, a small card file, a plastic file case with a few dozen folders for brochures and newsletters, and perhaps a special shelf for a few books and directories should be more than sufficient.

The Address Book

Use an address book with enough room to record names, phone numbers, addresses, and a few words to jog your memory about each person. The kind that allows you to replace pages is preferable; there is no need to buy a rococo system with color-coded pages, multiple pockets, and complicated headings. Most stationery stores still sell small notebooks with looseleaf sheets.

Tickler Files

Tickler files are a trick borrowed from sales professionals. The purpose of a tickler file is to remind you to call someone based on a date or deadline. Some network builders organize their tickler files by the dates they last talked to each person, with the first cards in the box being the oldest. Others organize the cards by month;

yet another technique is to "flag" cards that need attention with metal or plastic clips. And, finally, some people organize their files according to the anniversaries of the first time they met with each person.

If you are the kind of network builder who needs to keep in touch with a large number of people on an occasional basis, this system works well. You can make a simple tickler file by keeping a stack of file cards by your phone. When you talk to someone from one of your networks, note the person's name and phone number and the date on the card. If you flip through these cards once a month or so, you can readily see which connections are "aging" and need to be made current.

Dump Boxes

Dump boxes are the most user-friendly filing system ever devised. They strike terror in the hearts of many trained records managers, because they are sloppy and sometimes wrong, but they work fine for the average collection of brochures, flyers, and other materials that defy normal classification but need to be distributed quickly.

Simply dump your third class mail, extra brochures, and other printed material that you want to share with your network into one or more large wire baskets. You can use several wire baskets and devise some kind of rough classification system, but the idea is not to have 37 color-coded boxes with detailed labels. Then let everyone dig for themselves. The "rummage sale" flavor attracts many people who would otherwise be shy about going through the standard vertical filing systems that are a staple of most libraries. There is no order to disrupt or materials to refile. Post a sign to encourage people to take what they want. If someone happens to ask to empty all of the baskets for her own complex filing systems, say yes, with your blessings. There will always be materials to take the place of whatever she carts away.

Bulletin Boards

A well-managed bulletin board is a delight and, in many circumstances, is the preferred network builder's information distribution system:

> It can be placed in high traffic areas
> It is accessible to everyone in the institution
> It can be scanned quickly

It educates many people about information exchange by example

It is simple, inexpensive, and flexible

Card File Systems

Everyone has their own way of organizing their address book or personal filing system. Just remember that you can run a successful network-building project with a recipe card box and a package of index cards.

Two pieces of information are essential to successful network building: the date you first met a person and how you met them—through an introduction from a mutual friend, a note in a newsletter, a conference or workshop, etc. This data is often left out of the homegrown system. It is invaluable when you need to trace the connections among a network, give credit for a referral, or measure the effectiveness of an ad or publicity story.

What about a Computer?

Designing a database is a subject that takes up entire walls of books in large bookstores and libraries. The best advice is to wait until you absolutely must have one or else, and then put it off another six months. The only exception to the rule is if you happen to fall into one of a few specific categories:

1. Your school already has an integrated computer database package that is relatively easy to use and you have students who can design and manage a system for you at no extra cost to the school.

2. You are married to or the parent of a computer genius who will design the ideal system for you for free and keep it running at no cost.

3. You love designing and maintaining computer databases as a kind of mental health hobby, but you promise you will not let the computer get in the way of your network activities.

4. You find some other organization with the money, time, personnel, and long-term stability to manage your records for you at a small cost.

5. You are part of some large, well-financed educational institution that already has a system used to maintain subscription lists, etc.

Outside of these exceptions, a computer system is not recommended for most network-building activities, at least not for the first few years.

The Network Directory

Most network builders at one point or another succumb to the allure of the directory. There are many reasons to believe that a directory is necessary to build good relationships with people. You may tell yourself that if only you had one place to find the information you needed for your projects, you would become more efficient at solving problems. Projects with small budgets could receive better exposure. Duplication of efforts could be eliminated because everyone would have the same information.

Remember, an archive is not the same as a network. A directory creates a dated snapshot of organizations and people who are interested in the particular idea that is the focus of the network. The snapshot is accurate only as long as the information is valid and relatively complete.

Two groups are affected by the success of a directory. First are the people who are listed in the directory. They want publicity for their projects and ideas. Second are the people who use the directory. They want solutions for their problems. The first group wants detailed listings with complete information about their projects and, if they pay for their space, some guarantee that they will get their money's worth out of their participation. The second group wants a well-designed and well-indexed directory that is easy to use and will stay up-to-date as long as possible.

In addition, there are internal directories and external directories. Internal directories are used inside an institution or organization to allow people to know about each other and take advantage of each other's skills and abilities. The listings might include professional information, including degrees, work history, current position, and job responsibilities, and personal information, focusing on family, hobbies, and skills. External directories are used to promote projects and individuals among many organizations and are often available to the general public.

If you want to produce a directory, keep in mind the following general caveats:

1. Directories go out of date very quickly. One rule of thumb used in the publishing industry says that a directory will be 1–5 percent out of date on the day it is published. In one national directory used for research for this book, 20 percent of the contact information was incorrect, and 5 percent of the entry subjects had vanished completely. This directory was less than a year old, and all of the entries had been checked within a few months of publication.

2. Updating directories and publishing the results is a costly effort in terms of both money and personnel.

3. A directory can become a red herring. The people who are not included in the directory can be overlooked, even if they deserve attention and respect.

4. A directory can become the focus of a political battle, with various groups upset that their projects were not included.

5. Organizations and individuals listed in directories can become targets for unwanted pitches from salespeople and fundraisers. This is true of both internal and external directories. A disclaimer that instructs the reader not to use the directory to violate other people's privacy will be ignored by the unscrupulous.

6. Directory listings can be incorporated into other directories without the permission of those listed. If any errors were printed in the original listing, those errors will be duplicated.

7. Directories are never used as much or as well as the publishers desired.

8. External directory publishers who give the directories away for free in the hope that the audience will pay for subsequent issues are usually disappointed.

9. Directories are rarely well distributed or well publicized. This is true even of internal directories.

If you still insist on having a directory for your networking project, consider the following ideas to improve its longevity and usefulness.

1. Decide how the directory will be distributed and how updates will be financed before you design the format and begin soliciting entries.

Who needs to receive a copy in order for the directory to be useful? Will distribution be done through preset distribution channels? If so, does the design of your directory meet the requirements of the distribution organization?

2. Decide what form the directory needs to take.

Would a newsletter with current listings published on a quarterly basis be more useful than one ponderous telephone directory issued once a year? Would an internal directory be more useful if it were designed as an online database with employee access? Or would a well-managed bulletin board do the same job as printed pages? What if the directory was published as an insert in the local newspaper?

3. Send everyone whose information is entered in the directory a written confirmation so they can check for errors.

If that is not possible, make sure the information you extract from other sources is correct. Never rely on the accuracy of the printed word.

4. Set specific guidelines as to length and format of each entry and stick to them.

The longer the entry, the less likely it will be read and used. The most useful directories have between 25 and 50 words of text per entry.

5. Do not make any promises to the people listed in the directory concerning how publication of the directory will affect their organization.

Discourage anyone who believes that the publication will save a failing project by creating a sudden storm of interest and donations.

6. Make sure that the listings contain information that can be made public.

Discourage people from putting their home phone numbers or addresses into any print publication. There is no way you can guarantee that a printed directory (or a computerized one, for that matter) might not fall into the wrong hands. Encourage any organizations without an office to get a post office box and use an answering service.

7. The organization or person responsible for sending in the listing should make some determination of how long the current contact information will remain valid.

If any major changes are anticipated within one year of the directory's publication, such changes should be noted. Often school- and professional-related organizations are created in an academic setting and fall under a particular department. It is difficult for the casual reader to be certain whether the organization is a permanent part of the department or is the special project of the professor or staff person mentioned in the contact information. This should be clarified.

8. Encourage individuals with special interests to be specific about what they want to say about themselves and about what kind of replies they want to elicit from their entry.

There is a difference between what might called a "passive" entry and an "active" entry in a network directory. A typical passive entry might read:

I am interested in gardening, foreign languages, and travel.

An active entry might read:

I am collecting information on how to start and maintain a wildflower garden. In addition, I need to keep my German language skills up to par and need fluent, native speakers with whom to practice. Finally, I would like to swap my experiences backpacking in Europe with people who have climbed the highest peaks in the Canadian Rocky Mountains.

9. Avoid keywords; they mostly do not work.

A keyword entry in a directory lists a string of words, with no explanation, that are supposed to indicate a person's or organization's interests. If the directory has a specific focus, such as people who teach foreign languages, keywords can be useful. What is not useful is a stream-of-consciousness approach that might look like this:

economics, gardening, money, trip to Europe, back pain, Russian, special education.

Is the person interested in speaking Russian, teaching Russian, or meeting other Russian immigrants? What kind of gardening? And what flavor of economics?

A Sample Directory Format

All organizational entries in a network-building directory should contain the following information:

1. The full legal name of the organization

Any connections with other organizations, such as a university, city agency, or teachers' union, should be made clear. Sometimes, an organization will use someone's office as a mailing address; it is important to clarify whether a legal connection exists between the activities of the two organizations listed in the mailing address or title.

2. The name and title of the contact person

Since the world changes and people leave their jobs, organizations should establish titles or departments that do not change, even if the personnel does. Will someone who sends in for information five years after the directory is published receive a prompt response? Some organizations list both the name of the person and the name of the position. Marketing specialists encourage their client organizations to use the most important title they can in advertisements to encourage responses. People like to write directly to the president or the vice-president in charge of marketing.

3. The date of the entry

If all of the information for the directory was submitted about the same time, it is adequate to include frequently in the body of the directory a statement such as, "This is the 1992 directory; all submissions were received by November of 1991." Some organizations put a disclaimer in their entries, such as, "This information is accurate through 1993." Don't use vague terms like "the end of this year," because you don't know when the respondent will pick up a copy of the directory.

4. The full mailing address

Unless your organization has a long-term lease on your building or has a rock-bottom secure relationship with a significant agency or school system, use a post office box as your mailing address. If you use a street address, some people *will* show up in person. It is not unheard of for a school teacher who is setting up a formal network to list her school as the mailing address, only to be called out of class at the insistence of some member of the public who shows up during the day to talk to her. If someone wants to send you a package via one of the courier express services that requires a street address, the service will call or write you to obtain a street address.

5. The business phone number

Unless the organization is well established, the business phone might be the home phone of one of the people involved in the network. This saves money for the organization, but it precludes the organization being listed in the phone book or with directory assistance. You might decide how much you will save each month by calculating the difference in cost between a residential line and a business line, and then estimate the number of interested people who will be unable to find you if you are not listed. If you use a home number or a shared phone line, leave a clear message on a working answering machine indicating that callers indeed have reached the correct number.

Stability is important when you are building networks; most cities have reasonably priced answering services that allow you to keep the same phone number for a long time. Some organizations set up a phone and an answering machine in the office of a stable community organization such as a church.

6. The hours that the organization operates an office

Small network organizations are often parttime affairs with volunteer staff. It makes more sense to try to be open every Wednesday evening from 6:00 p.m. to 10:00 p.m. than to ask people to try "any time" in a hit-or-miss fashion.

7. The mission statement or some succinct statement of purpose—the best of these contain no jargon and are less than 25 words long

8. The cost of participating

9. The cost of receiving a sample packet of information

10. The kinds of queries the organization would welcome

11. The kinds of requests the organization does not handle

12. Pointers to other organizations and activities with allied interests

The Network Newsletter

The major difference between a directory and a newsletter is the relative frequency of publication. The measure of success for a network newsletter, as with the directory, is its ability to encourage readers to take action and contact each other. To that end, the majority of entries are short, preferably less than 50 words.

The hardest task of a newsletter editor is paring down submissions to fit what some contributors will feel are arbitrary submission guidelines. Practice being both friendly and firm when someone complains that his or her entry was gutted by your efforts to squeeze a 30-page dissertation into a single paragraph. You don't want to discourage the flow of information, but you need to be persuasive in a positive way about how the information is delivered.

Many newsletter editors have a straightforward solution to the problem of overly long submissions. They produce a simple, one-page handout with the answers to the most commonly asked questions about submitting information to the publication. Written guidelines work except when they become another manifestation of the bureaucratic mind. Your guidelines and submission forms should encourage people to send valuable information, not punish them for not following your guidelines. And if someone does send information on the back of a napkin written in crayon, thank them for the information, and *then* ask them if they could follow the guidelines the next time.

If your intention is to build a network among a diverse population, including parents, community leaders, senior citizens, students, and members of the general public, it is important to remember that many of your best contributors may not have good writing skills. They may be ashamed of their ability to handle English, or they may be functionally illiterate. If you are a teacher, be aware that a major complaint voiced by nonschool personnel about the teaching profession is the tendency of some teachers to treat other adults like children. Some submissions to the newsletter may be less than perfect, but this is not the time to tell a parent his or her grammar is terrible or to lecture the head of a community organization about spelling.

Encouraging a diversity of contributions means being flexible in how you receive information. For example, you may need to allow people to submit information over the phone. If you are dealing with a broadly based community, many potential contributors might not have any other way to submit information. Notice the increase in the use of "answer-back" phone lines by newspapers and radio stations. The media is discovering that many people would rather pick up the phone than write a letter.

Use an answering machine with the capability to play back messages several times, if need be, to help you transcribe contributions. Some people use a certain number just for phone messages about the network or publication; it is separate from the phone number used to make calls or to receive other kinds of messages. Also, you can control the flow of information somewhat by adhering to a "phone diet" and not answering your phone during certain times of the day. The majority of people are gracious and understanding when asked to call back during certain hours. On the other hand, your phone message policy should be like any other policy: It is there to keep you from burning out while you offer the best quality of service, not to punish people who need to break the rules because of an emergency or a change in plans.

Encouraging people to contribute may also mean allowing them to drop off information at one or more locations convenient to the community. Mailing a letter can be a burden to an elderly pensioner on a fixed income. You can take advantage of the natural gathering places in the community, such as a drug store, a community church, a public library, a community center, a popular record store, a senior center, a bookstore, a laundromat, a diner, a feed store, a recreation center, or even a doctor's office. Within a school building, a location that is convenient for teachers might not be convenient for custodians or the kitchen staff. Several clearly marked submission boxes can be used to collect contributions and promote your network-building activities. You can and should delegate the gathering of this information back to your network of contributors.

Distribution of Newsletters and Directories

The simple network guideline for distributing newsletters and directories is to make distribution part of the "cost" of participation. Some organizations are delighted to receive free directories to distribute to their own membership. In addition, individuals can take several and hand them out to friends.

Honesty is the best policy when discussing the circulation of your materials. Ten thousand directories produced is not the same as ten thousand distributed. Stick to the facts when people ask you about the success of your venture; they will respect and trust you more in the long run.

8

Networking the Special Event

Putting on a special community event is the most public measure of your ability to build support networks. It also highlights your effectiveness at building links with the rest of the community. Most events are organized with multiple goals. If you are serious about creating and maintaining working relationships, one major goal must be to build trust and better communications among the organizers and staff of the event and between the organizers and the public. If you are going to put on a community fair, for example, reach out to include everyone in the community, not just the parents who are active in the PTA.

By creating opportunities for different members of the community to contribute and participate, you not only strengthen the ties between your school and the community, you also can put on a better event. To be sure, networking is not necessarily "efficient" or neat. If, for example, you decide to involve elementary school students in producing signs for a career day fair, the signs may not be absolutely straight and professional looking. On the other hand, giving students a chance to become part of the program in such a visible way certainly outweighs the lack of "professionalism" in the art.

Networking also helps you avoid potentially disastrous situations, such as the school that put on a successful outdoor school fair but neglected to contact area homeowners before the event. Residents without children were caught by surprise when dozens of cars began taking up parking places and eager fair-goers trampled their lawns and flower beds. The resulting bad feelings lasted for months, all because the organizers forgot about the importance of the geographic community.

Clarifying Your Purpose

The first step when planning any event is to clarify whether and why a special event is necessary in the first place. The excitement of planning and presenting a conference, community fair, talent night, fundraising dinner, or lecture series is addictive, but the best meeting planners and conference organizers in the business world ask their clients some hard questions before agreeing to participate. Your "bottom line" might be different from that of the average corporation, but you still owe it to yourself and your school to examine exactly why you are putting resources into a project. Here are some reasons why a network builder might hold a special event.

1. To raise money

Many school districts hold special events to raise money for special projects, such as scholarships, new books for the library, or new equipment, or to fund a trip for a class. The main advantage of conducting fundraising as a public event is being able to reach people who may want to support the school but don't have the time to do it personally. For example, many people might welcome the opportunity to contribute by buying a raffle ticket, even though they may not be able to attend the event themselves.

The disadvantage of public fundraising is the amount of time and energy it takes to raise money from individuals. Therefore, it is important to investigate the probable success of the event before you commit to it. Can you actually make enough money to justify the investment of time and resources? The head of a public library in a large city states that he often cannot justify using valuable resources to raise money from the public, since it is more efficient for him to go to government sources and large corporations. However, he recognizes the need to reach new groups and to give the community a feeling of ownership and power in the library system.

Not every fundraising situation is suited to the event method. A crisis that requires that a certain amount of money be raised in a short period of time might be better served by calling or visiting those special donors you know you can count on to help. The conventional wisdom among many professional fundraisers is that 80 percent of the funds come from 20 percent of the donors. By focusing on those 20 percent and involving them more intensely, by putting them on your advisory board, and by inviting them to participate in regular events, you can plug into the personal networks of wealthy and generous individuals who can contribute substantially to your cause.

This is an excellent example of one of the prime dilemmas of networking. Who are the "right" people to network with for a particular purpose? If you go after the wealthier and more influential individuals and organizations in your community, you may ensure financing for your projects, but you also risk alienating other individuals and groups, particularly among disenfranchised minorities, who are likely to feel left outside the inner circle of power and prestige. On the other hand, do you cripple your fundraising efforts by not relying enough on those with "deep pockets" who are waiting for someone to ask them for help?

Neither is the "right" solution. Network building is a long-term process that should combine both approaches. If you decide to see every member of the community as a potential problem solver, you can grow connections into all parts of your community. You also will avoid creating a situation where the people running a community organization are of a significantly different ethnic, racial, and/or socioeconomic status than the people whom the organization is supposed to serve.

In the field of school-community relations, it is especially important not to assume that the obvious leaders in the community are the only ones who can help. A family of modest means that feels a commitment to the school may actually contribute more than a wealthier family whose resources are going to help a dozen different causes.

2. To publicize the school to the community

Before planning a publicity event, you need to answer three questions:

How will you define the community you want to reach?

What exactly about your school do you want to publicize?

Why do you want to publicize by means of a special event?

To define your community, look at the networks of children and adults both inside and outside of your school. If you are planning to invite families of staff members, make sure you include *everyone* on the staff, not just teachers and other fulltime, degreed professionals. An all-school event means just that; never, ever decide for other people whether they would want to attend an event—ask them.

Outside your school, the parents are the first group that comes to mind. But what about the other adults and children in the neighborhood of your school building? If you are trying to present a good image of your school, you cannot rely only on the connections you have through formal parent organizations. This is especially true of school districts where children are bused out of their neighborhood and attend schools many miles from their homes. Many parents face the same dilemma as the public school teacher in an inner-city school whose daughter makes the daily 34-mile round trip from her ethnically mixed neighborhood to a white suburb across town. The parent's sense of connection with her daughter's school has been eroded by distance. The school's community of parents spans several neighborhoods. All of these adults have some stake in the welfare of the school, but they are not likely to meet one another at the grocery store or the neighborhood park.

"Stakeholder" is a new concept in business that extends the definition of people who have a say in a business's financial and community activities. The concept is reaching into the schools and is worth considering, particularly as the tax implications of public schools affect more people without children. Has anyone done a survey of the adults in your immediate neighborhood to determine how many of them have children in your school or in other schools? How many are retired or living on fixed incomes? How many have no children? Yet these people are likely to have a say in the next school bond issue or on the acquisition of a new parking lot or playground.

You may discover that most of the people who are being asked to control the fate of your school do not have children in attendance. Shouldn't they be considered part of your community? How about the local firefighters and police officers, the owners of the small businesses in the vicinity of your building, and the people who work in nearby highrises?

Once you have defined your audience, identify exactly what you want to publicize. Some schools simply want the community to know that they are alive and well. Others are hoping to head off bad publicity by showing off the achievements of students and staff to a skeptical or unaware public. And still others are trying sell the value of the schools in preparation for a bond election.

Once you decide who and what, ask why an event is the best way to achieve your goals. A special event brings people together. That in itself is enough reason in some circumstances to go to the trouble. Perhaps it is time for the participants in the networks you have been carefully weaving to meet each other. If so, your special event may have the flavor of a family reunion, particularly if there is some way for people to identify those who previously were only voices on the phone.

In this age of sound bites and instant replays, a special event can also be a means to offer something of value to the media. Television stations love to film children and broadcast the clips during news shows, for the simple reason that the children, the parents and other family members, the neighbors, and everyone else who is part of the personal network will want to watch the broadcast. On slow news days, which are frequent in the late summer, during the holidays, and on weekends, news assignment editors sometimes have to scramble for footage. Your event can be a welcome blessing for a television or radio staff.

3.   To publicize a special program of the school

Educational programs where students perform, such as in theater, music, and sports, form a good basis for special events. An open house to show off the new computer lab can be fun if you are able to stock a few games and have enough skilled fifth graders on hand to guide adults the mysteries of modern technology.

4.   To entice parents to come to school

How do you get parents to come to school for an event, particularly when so many households are managed by adults who work outside the home fulltime? Do what businesses are doing: Sell the event in a way that is compatible with the needs of the parents. To market their wares to today's working parents, retail stores stay open late, offer food and day care on the premises, provide convenient parking or valet service, and schedule events over several days.

It is important for schools to communicate information about special events several times. Murphy's Law dictates that the day the flyers about the parent conference are distributed, half the children will lose their flyers in puddles. A calendar should be mailed to each household at the beginning of the year, with flyers mailed and delivered during the year to reinforce the information.

If you are not sure how to get parents to come to your school, why not ask them? The answers might surprise you. Some parents might tell you that they feel unwanted by the school or that they do not possess the appropriate wardrobe or right education. Some might tell you that their opinions are not wanted. Others are harboring fears left over from their own bad experiences in school. One elementary school teacher says that some of her parents turn "green around the gills" during parent conferences because they have such bad memories of their own elementary school experiences. A few phone calls and a willingness to listen can solve many such marketing problems.

5. To improve the image of the school

Public relations specialists warn that promotion and advertising can only be put in place when you know what you are trying to accomplish. This means research and evaluation, a step lamentably absent from many public relations programs.

Perhaps you have heard from people in your community networks that the school has a "bad reputation." What, exactly, do they mean? Experience has shown that people who are dissatisfied are more likely to voice their feelings than people who are pleased. If one high-decibel dissenter influences overlapping networks of people, the noise from that person's criticisms can create the impression of widespread dissatisfaction. Before you launch a campaign to improve your school's image, first find out what that image is among several diverse networks. Don't be surprised if the information you receive is as diverse as the populations your school serves.[1]

6. To create a feeling of community in the neighborhood

A great way to create a sense of community is to give a group of people a common project to tackle, one with tangible results and a fixed time for completion. A good example is the annual Work Day that used to be held at Goddard College in Vermont. Classes were suspended, and everyone, from the longtime president, Royce "Tim" Pitkin, to the newest student, worked together on a variety of construction and landscaping projects around the campus. In the evening a big picnic was held to celebrate the end of a tiring but satisfying day.

If you are planning a special event to generate community, you might consider a day that brings people together to build something tangible then reward them with food and entertainment.

7.   To create support around community issues (e.g., drugs, graffiti, gangs, dropouts)

One of the more popular events in one of the worst drug- and gang-ridden neighborhoods of a major Midwestern city is an annual appreciation day for the law enforcement officials who work to make the community a decent place to live. During the day, government officials and ministers stand in line for barbecue and cake with street people, children, and members of rap groups. Everyone is cheerful, the food is lavish, and the music is appropriately loud. Every other person in attendance seems to be a police officer, a firefighter, or a paramedic. Many bring their families to enjoy the excellent food and the special demonstrations. The firefighting equipment and the mounted police on their shiny Morgan horses are crowd favorites.

What kind of event could you plan for your school that would involve many different networks of professionals, average citizens, children, and community leaders?

8.   To honor an individual or group of individuals

There is a trend away from lavish dinners, award banquets, and memorial services and toward special events that make a positive impact in the general community. If you want to pay tribute to a favorite teacher or a beloved school administrator, you might forget the chicken pot pie and the cash bar and, instead, plant a grove of young trees or have a naming ceremony for a community-school garden. Or, if the dinner is a required or traditional event, you could follow the example set by the members of one student council. They voted to serve the adults at a school board dinner a "poverty-level" meal of the kind of food normally available through government surplus programs. The money left over was donated to a poverty program.

9.   To create a forum for discussion

Gove Community School in Denver runs a successful program of classes, seminars, and summer camps aimed at families throughout the city. During the last few years, the school has instituted a series of public town meetings. These programs have succeeded in part because the administrators of the school are terrific at building networks with other organizations and at setting high standards for the level of discussion at the programs. Big and difficult issues are tackled, and the discussions are anchored by well-known and credentialed experts.

In a program addressing the recent war in the Persian Gulf and the draft, panelists included representatives from Selective Service, the American Friends Service Committee, the armed forces, veterans groups, and student groups. Topics included registering for the draft and how to be a conscientious objector. Audience participation was designed into the program, and the event was well publicized.

Planning a public forum such as this does contain some pitfalls, which you will want to avoid. These include:

A failure to include diverse opinions
Omitting significant community organization participation
Poor publicity, particularly in mainstream publications
A structure that does not allow audience feedback

All of these problems can be addressed by means of existing and new networks.

Using Your Networks To Make the Decision

Use your networks to help make the decisions about why your school or school community should stage an event. Some of the issues on which your connections can give you feedback include:

1. Topics or themes

2. Times, dates, and places

Check for religious holidays and conflicts with other groups and organizations. The Junior League, the local United Way, the mayor's office, a convention bureau, or the local newspaper often have calendars that include the events of other organizations.

3. Admission price, if any

This can be a touchy subject in schools where there is a significant disparity among the incomes of families. Many schools harbor a "secret" group of poverty-level families who appear to be solidly middle-class, but are actually living close to the edge. Most students will be honest and accurate about how much their families can afford to spend; remember to include them in the decision making.

4.   How to address the needs of groups such as the handicapped, the elderly, working parents, students, the homeless, and the institutionalized

You won't be able to please everyone, but you can take into consideration whether a building can handle wheelchairs and when an event might be scheduled to be most convenient to the majority of working parents. Too many schools still hold important conferences and public events during weekdays when parents are unable to attend. Unfortunately, coping with working families also means longer hours for school personnel, an issue most school systems are not addressing.

5.   Whom to "officially" invite, such as the county commissioners; the heads of the local political parties; the commissioner of education; corporate, civic, and religious leaders; and representatives from other schools

This is where your network can save you from the embarrassment of inviting only the establishment leaders. Your map of the cultural and ethnic networks in your community can help you plan for any special invitations. The one question you cannot ask too many times is, "What and whom are we forgetting?" If you use your network contacts well and make a good faith effort to keep the process open to community input through well-publicized planning meetings, published phone numbers, and easily accessible contact people, you will find that mistakes are usually forgiven, or at least put in context.

The Focus Group

One of the most successful tools of the business world is the focus group. Very simply, a representative group of individuals is invited to share their opinions under the direction of a trained facilitator. In a relaxed setting with beverages, snacks, and sufficient time to talk, the facilitator asks questions and engages the participants in a frank discussion of the product, service, or issue being explored.

This model is a useful way to use your networks when planning a large community event. You might not like what the participants say about your ideas, but the information will be honest and useful. The purpose of the focus group is not to plan the event, but to reveal ideas, opinions, and feelings to which you might not otherwise have access.

Planning the Event

Once the event committee is satisfied that a special event is a good idea, use your network connections to build the teams that can put the event together. Many excellent books on running special events include detailed information on budgeting, site preparation, and catering.[2] This section is about the details that such books leave out—finding volunteers, money, and other contributions.

Finding Volunteers

The key to incorporating volunteers, particularly community volunteers, into your event is having a realistic assessment of which tasks must be under the control of paid professionals or within the core group of organizers and which tasks can be delegated. (Insurance and legal restrictions will, to some extent, dictate what you can or can't do in your locality.) It is important to remember that strengthening your working relationships with the community inside and outside the school is often as much a part of the goal as getting the job done perfectly. And don't assume that "volunteer" has to mean "sloppy" or "amateurish." Every community contains many professional, but underutilized, volunteers.

Students and Other Overlooked Resources

In some schools, students are always respected participants in events, while in others they are ignored as possible contributors. In some communities, for example, high school students, either as part of an advanced Red Cross first-aid class, a 4-H club, or a local scout troop, run the first-aid tent with adult supervision. Many children are also quite capable of managing basic financial information and coping with budgets and bookkeeping, usually at a younger age than adults are willing to accommodate.[3]

Other overlooked volunteers and participants in the school

institution include school custodians, bus drivers, and retirees, as well as neighborhood adults without children in the school, small-business owners, public employees, and individuals who are not part of any formal group or organization. The disenfranchised in your geographical network are numerous enough for you and your planning committee to assume that this is a time to "network everybody."

Posters and press releases announcing that you are looking for volunteers usually are not very effective. Better ideas include personal appeals at other people's meetings, radio and television public service announcements, and calling on people one-to-one. The best way to recruit volunteers is through volunteers who are already working with you and are enjoying the experience.[4]

Formal network generators such as service clubs, churches, professional associations, corporations, businesses, and recreational clubs often like to take on special projects; their members are trained and experienced at putting on events. You might call local meeting planning organizations to see if you can get some expert advice as a donation.

If you and others on the events committee keep coming up with the same 20 names, this is evidence that your efforts to reach into the diverse communities in your school district leave something to be desired. Even a small town can suffer from the "parallel networks syndrome." This happens when individuals in close proximity occupy networks that don't seem to touch or overlap, usually because of profoundly different world views or values. Parallel networks can be separated by race, socioeconomic status, religion, or lifestyle. Remember to ask yourself, "Who are we leaving out?" A random search through the phone book can help you break out of this syndrome in your own volunteer recruiting efforts.

Finding Money and Contributions

Use the same rules to locate funding and donations for your event as you do in looking for volunteers. Ask everyone, particularly people who are not being asked "because." Ignore the "because" and ask. This is a good time to play "Random Walk." Ask the most unlikely people on your list for contributions of money, donated goods, or services. Remember: People who don't ask don't receive. Let other people decide to turn you down; don't anticipate a no and decide not to call them in the first place.

The Network Approach to Marketing Your Event

The network approach to reaching your audience before an event goes beyond the usual advertising and promotion. The key is to identify formal organizations and enlist their aid in telling their constituencies about the event. This can be as simple as asking local community centers if you can post flyers on their bulletin boards or if they will include your flyers in their mailings to members. It might include a spokesperson showing up at other groups' meetings to explain the event and ask for help in some form. It might mean asking for sponsors or partners who will lend their name or provide funds in exchange for publicity. It might even mean combining efforts and creating joint events with other groups, including combining programs that formerly were held separately.

The difference between this kind of marketing and using the normal public channels is that you are capitalizing on existing relationships with specific, targeted audiences. It takes some time to locate the appropriate groups and, in many cases, to go through the proper channels to work with them. Also, you need enough lead time to take best advantage of printing and meeting schedules and to work around holidays, vacations, and the two major downtimes for many groups: the summer vacation months and the months of November and December, when many people are busy with the winter holidays and their own special programs.

Here are a few tips on how to make your network marketing more successful:

1. Assign one person from your school and one from the other group to be responsible for the contacts between the two organizations.

2. Make sure that both work and home numbers are available for each contact person and that phone numbers of "backup" people are available in case of an emergency.

3. Set specific goals and deadlines and keep to them.

4. Make sure that each group you choose for this network marketing approach gets the exposure they want.

During the Event

Network building does not stop when the event starts. Any event should be designed so that participants have time to converse with each other. Community events should facilitate the mixing of people from many segments of the community; part of your success is getting unlikely people talking with each other!

Internal and External Media Relations

Media relations refers to the way information is communicated both to participants and to the greater community by means of the normal media outlets. During a major event, you will need to know how emergency announcements will be distributed for such normal crises as lost children, car lights left on, a change in plans because of the weather, or a change in the schedule. Even a small parent-teacher council meeting needs a message system so that attendees are not out of touch with their homes and offices.

Media professionals will appreciate your assigning a knowledgeable person with some authority and decision-making capacity to meet their needs. The media liaison can schedule photo opportunities, round up likely people for print interviews, and set up special happenings with plenty of colorful action and sound for the television crews. Media people always need a phone to check with their assignment editors. They also appreciate being provided with refreshments.

The Network Booth

Most events include some sort of information and messaging center. Make the center a more useful tool for network building by including a public message area, a knowledgeable staff, literature about your school, information about event cosponsors, and a way for people to get in touch with other attendees during and after the event. The booth should have:

1. A well-done map of the event, posted with large type and copied for distribution. This is a must for street fairs and programs involving more than a few exhibits.

2. A directory of participating groups, with appropriate names, addresses, phone numbers, and contact information, which is available for distribution. You can create another directory

to distribute after the event by having a sign-up sheet available for individuals representing groups or themselves who want to be part of a school-community directory.

3. A place where participants can leave each other notes. At a regional education conference, attendees were photographed with an "instant" camera when they registered; the photographs were posted on a message board with information about each person and the organization he or she represented. A space was left by each photo for other attendees to leave notes.

Event Hosts

Another kind of staff person is the one who wanders through the crowds offering assistance to attendees. At the average event, this kind of helper focuses on finding lost purses, leading sunburned participants to the first-aid tent, and settling differences between the occupants of adjoining booths. A network helper, called a host or network "weaver," is more likely to overhear a conversation between two participants about a need for volunteer programs and point them to the appropriate booth.

Network hosts are useful at conferences to encourage newcomers to mingle with "old-timers" and to gently, but insistently, break up some of the cliques that inevitably form. They are more than traffic cops and often have as much information to share as the keynote speaker. When recruiting hosts for your event, you need to look for three qualities or three kinds of hosts.

People with Expertise

People with expertise in their field might include experienced teachers and staff members from inside the school or consultants with special skills in areas like respite care, literacy, gifted and talented children, music education, or languages. They are encouraged to talk to participants and to answer their questions. Before the program, they meet with the other hosts and, if appropriate, are introduced to the audience. They wear tags that identify their specialties and take turns staffing the network booth.

People with Strong People Skills

People with strong people skills are the ones who feel comfortable going up to strangers and starting a conversation. They are sent to look for wallflowers and introduce them to other people at the event. At multi-cultural events, they are likely to be bilingual or conversant in sign language. The goal of these hosts or weavers, if they are recruited only for their social skills, is to ensure that everyone attending the event is greeted in a friendly manner by an "official" of the school and made to feel glad that they have come.

People Who Like To Network

The network builders who act as host or weaver are the ones who carry phone lists, Rolodexes, and address books. They are armed with information about all the other network hosts. They don't pretend to know the answer to everything, but they are certainly willing to find out who does. They act as scouts, steering participants to the appropriate resources.

If you can find all three qualities in one person, you are lucky. It is not impossible, however. Good network builders often are also social people with a strong depth of knowledge and experience in at least one area. At a large event, the hosts can make the difference between a good event and a truly successful network-building event. In addition to having designated hosts, it may also be a good idea to have school personnel and other participants wear informational, funny, and comment-provoking name tags.

Recruiting for the Next Project

While the event committee is focused on making the current event a success, at least one member of your team should be thinking about how to use the event to gather names of new volunteers and contributors for the next event. This person might be the one assigned to making sure that someone is taking down the names, addresses, and phone numbers of participants and attendees. You may want to have a sign-up area or have a couple of volunteers with clipboards move around asking people if they would like to be notified of the next event and be offered a chance to volunteer.

After the Event

For the serious network builder, the work is only half over after the event is finished. The event itself, along with its other goals, was a time for participants to make new contacts and strengthen old ones. Now you need to turn your attention to making sure the contacts you made before the event were well treated and were satisfied with their participation in the event. You have information to gather and sift through from dozens of sources, and you must put it in some usable form for use in your school and, when appropriate, to share with the rest of the community. Many groups wisely assign these duties to a fresh team of people who are not burned out.

What are the duties of this special group of network builders who work after the event is over?

Documenting Participation

During the event, at least one person should work the crowd, mingling with the audience during intermissions and asking participants how they think the event is going. Are people happy? Is parking adequate? What would they like improved or changed? How did they hear about the event? Would they come the next time? This information is priceless, and rarely does a group take the time to collect it. Once collected, the information must be tabulated and analyzed. Also, each and every donation of time, money, and resources must be documented. This serves as a record and guide for future events, as well as providing a list for thank-you notes or phone calls.

Sharing the Results

Once the information is documented, you need to decide what to pass on to different individuals and groups inside and outside the school community. Every major contributor deserves a report of some kind. But other groups may need or want to see evaluations, demographics, attendance records, and information on who liked what the best. Also, you will have names, addresses, and phone numbers of potential volunteers and links with other networks. This is one instance where a computer with a database management system can reduce the time needed to deal with this information from weeks or months to hours or days.

The Importance of Volunteer Recognition

Maybe you grew up in the kind of family where you were not allowed to play with a new toy until you had written a thank-you note to the giver. A similar rule should apply to events. It is important to thank all of the volunteers as soon after the event as possible. One volunteer at an international educational conference, an event she had worked on for a year, received a letter of thanks *seven months* after the event. Needless to say, she turned her energies to helping another organization.

A potluck dinner where people can blow off steam, a party at the home of the event coordinator, a T-shirt ("I survived the Lincoln Middle School Annual Art Fair"), a funny pin, a mention in the report, a personal letter from the principal or school board president, a surprise appreciation luncheon, a plaque, a candy bar wrapped with a thank-you note, an ad in the local paper, or a banner in the hall of the school are all ways to show your appreciation to the people and organizations who helped.

The planning for the thank yous needs to begin with the first event meeting, so that money, resources, and people are budgeted to deal with them. Convince your team that these thank yous are a crucial investment in the success of future events and that they should be generous in their budgeting. It might be useful to designate one donor or group of donors as the "volunteer support team" and have their contributions be earmarked for the post-event thank yous.

Maintaining Your Networks

Most event organizers will tell you that a "post-party" depression sets in after a special event is over, particularly if it was planned and executed over a long period of time. The excitement is finished and it is time to get back to the daily routine. But wait— what about all of those people you met while you were planning the event whom you promised to call or write? What about the information you were supposed to send them? What about those individuals whom you did not have time to get to know, but with whom there was a mutual spark of interest and excitement?

A network builder once estimated that it would take 20 hours to follow through on all of the contacts made while attending the average conference. Your real work starts the week after the event. Make a phone call a day, write a postcard a day. By the end of a month, you should be on top of most of the contacts you promised to make, unless you have set unrealistic goals for yourself. There is no great secret to maintaining networks after an event. The personal contact is the key. Remember, the longer you wait, the more fragile those initial bonds will grow.

Networking at Other Peoples' Events

Here are some guidelines to remember if your school is contacted to participate in a community event and you find yourself in attendance or contributing time and labor.

1. Make sure you are clear with the other organization(s) about your own and your school's official obligations.

2. Keep tabs with the host organization about how many people are expected, whether donations and support are coming in on schedule, and the schedule for publicity.

3. Plan how your school can bow out gracefully if the host organization is unable to live up to its end of the bargain.

4. Send a responsible person to every planning meeting to represent your school and to report back on problems and progress.

5. Recruit your own volunteer staff ahead of time, with backup people just in case.

6. Check out the site before the event and make sure you will receive technical support as promised.

7. Create an inexpensive flyer about your school with whatever message you are trying to promote and print more than enough.

8. Bring an emergency booth kit with masking tape, transparent tape, glue, scissors, crepe, rags, thread and needle, marking pens, batteries, safety pins, industrial tape, poster paper, paper table cloths (they are usually wrapped two to a package), water container, business cards, banner tape (in case they forget to make you a sign), snacks (in case they forget to get you lunch or dinner), your network directory, extra change for phone calls, toilet paper (for outdoor events that use portable toilets), and several blank pads of paper with pens and pencils. Staffing the best-prepared booth at the fair is a great way to meet people who were not as ready for the normal event disaster.

9. Keep your expectations modest, and be gracious when things don't turn out well.

10. Follow through with your own thank yous.

Notes

1. In *Community Control in Education: A Study in Power Transition* (Midland, MI: Pendell, 1978), a study of the accountability issues in the Detroit Public Schools reveals very different attitudes among positions held by community members, whose viewpoints are labeled as "militant black," "moderate," and "white establishment."

2. Some excellent manuals on event planning and community fundraising include: *Successful Community Fundraising: A How-To Manual* (Ottawa, IL: Caroline House, 1979), *The Fund Raiser's Guide to Successful Campaigns* (New York: McGraw-Hill, 1988), and *The Meeting Planners' Guide to Logistics and Arrangements* (Washington, DC: Institute for Meeting and Conference Management, 1986).

3. See Appendix C for several volumes that present both a practical and philosophical approach to involving children in "adult" activities.

4. In a national study on the subject, published as *Volunteer in Public Schools* (Washington, DC: National Academy Press, 1990), the authors reported that the best way to find volunteers was to ask existing, enthusiastic volunteers.

---------- 9 ----------

Creating a Community of
Network Builders

When network building works, it cannot help but inspire others. However, misinformation about networking can create barriers to integrating its practices into school institutions. After attending workshops on network building, a number of teachers and school media specialists have commented that, before the program, they thought networking was about getting ahead in their jobs by flattering principals and exploiting their colleagues. They express universal relief that the practice of networking is actually built on mutual aid.

Some people get "hooked" on networking for all of the right reasons. Being able to solve problems for others by making connections can empower each person involved in the transaction. The successful network builder feels useful and important; it is fun to be the person known as the one everyone comes to for help. But this attitude falls short of the goal of being a truly skilled communicator. The highest order of network-building competence is being able to influence others to improve and practice their own network-building skills.[1]

One measure of your success at inspiring others is when colleagues and students tell you they are using your techniques to solve their own problems. Part of your ongoing role is to encourage these efforts at bridge building without sounding patronizing. A simple "that's great" is sufficient. Welcome the fact that others might be successful with people who have turned you down. After all, different people have different communication styles and different agendas. Even though you might have more experience and success at building support networks, a newcomer's enthusiasm can make up for a lack of skill and finesse.

Signs of Success

What would your institution be like if most of the members of the school were good bridge builders? How would it be different from the way it is today? Here are descriptions of some occurrences that let you know members of your school community are learning to build their own useful relationships.

1. Your students don't have to be prompted to find experts to interview for a term paper.

They feel comfortable calling on university professors, business owners, community activists, and politicians for information and advice. The members of one high school media bureau became so aggressive about pursuing stories during a presidential campaign that they were able to "scoop" the major wire services, getting an exclusive interview with a celebrity campaigner. A student jumped into a moving limousine and taped an exclusive interview with actor Paul Newman. He then rushed back to school, edited the tape, and delivered it to the local radio station along with a written introduction, in time for the afternoon broadcast of his school's news show. During the same school year, one of his classmates borrowed some clothes from her mother and pretended to be an adult reporter while interviewing some members of the American Nazi Party during a demonstration.

2. Positive coverage of your school's activities becomes commonplace in the local media, and most of the stories are being placed by people other than you and the school-community affairs liaison.

3. You hear increasing mentions of staff members' involvement with nonschool organizations such as Toastmasters, the Rotary Club, and various business and neighborhood improvement groups.

4. During the planning of a school carnival, several committee members mention the need to solicit community participation and then follow up their suggestions with action.

5. Used-looking Rolodexes and file card boxes begin appearing on the desks of staff people throughout your school.

6. Newcomers to your school staff report that everyone made them feel especially welcome on their first day and that follow-up is terrific.

7. The bulletin board in the teachers' lounge is filled with current information placed by everyone on the staff, not just by the teachers and clerical staff.

8. You overhear a degreed professional seriously discussing a problem in educational philosophy with a maintenance worker.

9. You see an increasing number of parents and other adults from the community at the school during and after school hours—your school building is frequently mentioned as a logical place to hold meetings, and staff members are invited to more and more community functions.

At a public meeting on economic development, a teacher who is active in environmental and social concerns in her community discovered that education was the topic of one of the panels but that the panel did not include a single educator. She spoke up from the floor of the conference and, she feels, made a positive impact. Perhaps the next program organizer, she says, will invite teachers to participate.

10. More and more teachers are scheduling outside speakers for their classes on their own.

Personal referrals are the main way that teachers find speakers and resource people for their classes. By the same token, the successes you share with your colleagues can influence them to contact other people, particularly if you are generous in sharing your best classroom connections.

Passing It On

How can you inspire the teachers and staff people around you to think about reaching out? It starts with the behavior you demonstrate to others. Ironically, some information people are possessive about their skills. They are the ones who help give networking a bad name. You can avoid their errors by remembering that every member of the school community is a participant in your most important professional network and treating each person accordingly.

Give Credit Where It Is Due

Jane Ulrich, director of the Southwest Regional Library System in Colorado, does a great job of acknowledging the accomplishments of the school and public librarians she serves. In print and in personal conversations, she makes sure the people doing the work receive full credit. For example, when she received a compliment on some materials she distributed at her annual system conference, she immediately gave credit to the other system directors who had given her permission to use the information that they had collected.

Go out of your way, particularly in the beginning when you are building credibility for your efforts, to acknowledge people's contributions. If someone gives you a great idea for a project, remember to include his or her name when you present the finished report on the project. Make a point of letting other people know whose idea it was. In documents about a school project, include the names of the people who helped. When you work with groups and organizations outside the school community, most of them expect that the positive publicity they receive will be the major compensation for their involvement. Keep good notes so that you can be accurate with your public praise.

An important part of being credible with an acknowledgment is being specific. It builds your credibility when you take the time to remember both the person and the specific contribution.

Does it take extra time to acknowledge everyone? Yes. Is it worth it? *Yes.* This is particularly true of projects where people are volunteering their time and expertise.[2] Also, acknowledging the accomplishments of others is crucial in developing trust within organizations. A skilled network builder relies on past successes to continue to build a useful network for his or her school. After the novelty has worn off, an otherwise vital web of relationships can die if the people in the institution are not seeing their own efforts made visible and rewarded.

Say "Thank You"

Following are some simple, inexpensive ways to thank people for the time and effort they contribute to make your network work.

1. A written note on an amusing piece of stationery

A pad of yellow sticky notes with funny messages provides you a very inexpensive way to thank colleagues for their efforts. One elementary school teacher tries to jot down the funny or surprising things her students say to share later with their parents. And what about thanking your students? During traditional gift-giving seasons such as the winter holidays and the end of the school year, teachers are often swamped with presents. Children and their families would be delighted to receive acknowledgment for their gifts—and it sets a great example.

2. A phone call or personal visit to let your network participants know how they helped you

Remember the model of the three communication styles? For some people, a letter will never mean as much as a phone call. One middle school teacher makes a point of calling parents to compliment them on the behavior of their children in her classes. She will say something like, "Your son is very well mannered in class; you have done a wonderful job raising him. Thank you." She reports parents often call her principal to relay their pleasure at her calls, which only take a couple of minutes to complete.

An open house is another way to say thank you. Politicians have known for centuries that thanking supporters with a party is a great way to cement relationships. An afternoon "at home" with cookies and punch is one way to say thank you. If you do not have the room to invite people over, try meeting at someone else's home. Other possibilities include church basements, bars, coffeehouses, gymnasiums, condominium clubhouses, libraries, and public parks.

3. Making sure that other people know how much the members of your support network helped

Some organizations are plagued by negative gossip. For better or worse, human beings like to talk about each other; gossip helps people bond to one another by creating shared experiences, even if the experience is vicarious.[3] You can help make gossip a more benign and even healthy communication tool by spreading good things about people behind their backs. In addition to thanking people personally, let everyone else know that you think that person is terrific. This serves to create and strengthen trust in the group. It will work, however, only if your praise is sincere and believable.

This is a good tactic when Person A is trying to rebuild a relationship with Person B and Person B won't communicate with Person A. Saying nice things about Person B behind her back can have a positive influence on everyone involved.

4. Documenting the contributions of your network builders for their supervisors and sending copies of that documentation to the network builders

If a colleague makes a difference, make sure that a letter goes to his or her supervisor. At the same time, take the opportunity to praise the supervisor for his or her own support.

5. A very modest gift

Don Roberts of Minneapolis sells and rents films to the school and library communities. He is also a master gardener who includes a sprinkle of fresh herbs and garden seeds in each thank-you letter he sends. One popular bookstore prints bookmarks using children's artwork, which it obtains by sponsoring periodic contests. These bookmarks are given free to each customer. A simple and useful item like a bookmark promoting your school could be included with your thank yous.

A school media specialist finds out the favorite authors and topics of each person she wants to thank. She then either orders the books for the library (when appropriate) or obtains them through interlibrary loan. She says, straight-faced, that finding out the favorite authors of the principal is "one of the most important jobs of any school librarian."

6. A public thank you

A note on a bulletin board thanking the food service staff for their help with a nutrition unit is nice, but it is even nicer if you mention the participants by name and send a copy to your local paper. Many of the things people do for each other in your network can generate side benefits of personal and professional publicity. A public and official thank you, however, is not a substitute for a personal thank you. The personal thank you is always most important.

Thank You Essentials

All effective thank yous have some things in common.

1.   They are immediate.

A late thank you is better than no thank you at all, but best of all is the one that arrives promptly. For the network builder, this means having a handy supply of cards ready. The least expensive way is to buy prestamped postcards at the post office in bundles of 25.

2.   They are specific.

Even a form letter can have a handwritten note scribbled in the margin about a special contribution the recipient made to your project. This is a good time to remind a colleague of that special support he or she gave you. Even if it was done "in the line of duty," formal acknowledgment for the ride to the game or staying up to type a report means a great deal to the recipient.

3.   They are sincere.

A simple sentiment is fine if you mean every word. Be careful, particularly if you are sending out a number of thank-you notes to a group of people who know each other, not to use a rote sentence. If members of the group compare cards and find out that you wrote the identical "sincere" sentence on each, you might find some cold shoulders the next time you call for help.

4.   They make the recipient feel special.

Make the thank you personal, with an anecdote or some indication that you know the person's special interests. The person who sends liquor to a known teetotaler or a "cat card" to a notorious dog lover is missing the boat. This personal touch sounds phony and made up to some people, but this is the case only if it is not honest. If you really don't care about the people in your network and, consequently, don't want to take the time to learn and remember what is important to them, by all means, don't fake it. But having such an attitude will make it more difficult for you to build lasting support networks.

Share the Information

You will discover plenty of opportunities to share information even before you are asked, such as the following:

1.   The name of a great speaker who loves to give talks to children

2. The name of a local business owner who will look over the final version of a grant proposal to a foundation

3. A senior center director who has lots of eager volunteers ready to help on a variety of projects

4. Your media list

5. Copies of the brochure from the latest conference you attended

6. A new magazine

7. A personal tip on tax help

8. Information about a career opportunity

9. This book

Sharing information has three elements. First, make sure everyone in your network has the same accurate information about what you are trying to accomplish; second, practice what you preach; and third, know when and what *not* to share.

Make Sure Everyone Has the Same Information

Principal Tim Snyder and the staff and students at Ortega Middle School in Alamosa, Colorado, rely a great deal on the support of the community, and there are always visitors and parttime staff people in the building. The mission of the school is printed on big signs throughout the school for students, teachers, staff, and visitors to see. It is also printed on the various documents the school uses, including the business cards that staff members carry to use as networking tools throughout the school.

The mission statement is more than academic jargon. It reads "T.E.A.M.," which stands for Together Everyone Achieves More. If this was just an empty slogan, it would have no effect. But Snyder and his staff try to practice what they preach, from the middle school philosophy that combines a child-centered and knowledge-centered curriculum, to creating blocks of time so that team teachers can exchange information outside of class, to recruiting local experts and authorities to present specialized programs to the students.

In the Effective Schools Program, sponsored by the Bureau of Indian Affairs/Office of Indian Education Programs, a "clear mission statement" is the number one characteristic of an effective school, according to the research of the program. ("Home/school/

community relations" is also on the list of characteristics of an effective school.[4])

Practice What You Preach

You might think that someone who practices good communication would be generous about sharing facts, figures, and contacts. However, information is a powerful tool, and that power tempts some people to make their information exclusive.

An experienced elementary school teacher who works in the largest school district in her state reported an unfortunate trend. The proliferating competitions being held to honor excellence in the teaching profession have created unhealthy barriers among teachers. Because the awards are linked to cash prizes, prestige, career advancement, and favorable notice by the principal, teachers in some schools are reportedly refusing to share their best ideas with their peers. The rewards for not sharing ideas, and thereby creating a temporary monopoly and gaining a competitive edge, are greater than the rewards for working with other teachers. A high school teacher with almost three decades of experience agrees, offering the reminder that the most important reward in teaching is the love and respect of students.

Unhealthy competition can be eliminated if the administration, staff, and teachers of each school together agree to reward all kinds of excellence and make the sharing part of the award system for teachers and other employees. This way, school staff members whose achievements are masked by a quiet, craftsperson attitude toward their profession can look forward to the same kind of praise and support as their more innovative and assertive colleagues.

Know When Not To Share

Some information is not appropriate to share with others. A good network builder must also be good at keeping secrets. You will sometimes become the custodian of information that is not yours to reveal, including:

1   Information that you have promised not to share as a condition of your having access to it

2.   Personal information about another colleague

3.   Information you have paid for and that is not legally yours to share. This would include making unauthorized copies of

computer software or lending a mailing list that you rented for one-time use

4. Information about students, parents, and school families

You may have a valid concern about how a person who requests certain information might use it. In such cases, set some simple rules that give you some control over how the information is used. For example, if someone wants to use a mailing list you have compiled, ask to see a copy of the piece they intend to mail as a condition of their having access to the list. If the person requesting the information is someone you don't know very well, give them one name to contact from your list, then check to see if the conversation went as promised. This is a good way to screen for colleagues who want to use your connections to sell a product or service but misrepresent their intentions.

Ask for Help

After a workshop on building support networks in their own schools, a group of school media specialists was asked to write down what information they thought they could use immediately. Almost every participant cited the need to let other people be useful to them as the most important idea they learned at the workshop:

> "Let people do things for me more."
> "Rely on others for answers and help."
> "Be more receptive to help."
> "Spend more time asking kids what they want in a library."
> "Work on letting others be useful to me."
> "Don't be boring. . . . Let others help."

As pointed out in the chapter about network building in your school, sending the message that you are only a giver and never a taker is not congruent with the definition of a network or a network builder. Think of a measurable change you could make in your own behavior that would demonstrate to your colleagues that you are serious about sharing information. If you are having trouble coming up with something, ask someone who knows you well for suggestions. Then write down a goal based on the new behavior and begin to practice that behavior.

Some of the following behaviors might be appropriate for you to try:

1. Be quiet at a meeting (particularly if you are known as a talkative person).

2. Listen to someone's problem and ask her what she thinks she should do about it before you suggest an answer.

3. Admit that you don't know an answer and refer a request to someone else.

4. Make a point of asking friends for advice or ideas, especially if you think of yourself as the person with all of the answers.

Respect Others' Territories

As you demonstrate your willingness to share information, recognize the boundaries of other people's comfort zones. There are the obvious legal problems if, in your enthusiasm, you begin to violate copyright law or accidentally leak information to the media. But other boundaries also exist that must be respected. Many institutions, for example, have customs that have the force of law; these customs are difficult to bend. They might seem foolish or even harmful, but if you take a pick axe to them, you could risk alienating the very people you are hoping to win over.

Change is sweeping the school universe. Teachers and other school personnel face overwhelming and often conflicting demands and workloads that have increased markedly from one or two decades ago. Schools are now supposed to accomplish what used to be the role of the family. Teachers feel that students lack respect for them and for the system, while students, parents, and community leaders feel that teachers no longer care. Many educators are dealing with guilt, anger, and fear about being made scapegoats for the problems of society. In this atmosphere any change can be seen as threatening.

A school aide, trained to improve the nutrition of children in poverty programs, was assigned to a school lunch program in rural northern Vermont. She was horrified at the poorly designed menus of her untrained predecessor. In her desire to make a clean sweep, she forgot to make friends with the kitchen staff or praise them for the difficult job they had in creating edible meals out of a limited budget and the unimaginative stocks of government issue food in their cupboards. Also, she neglected to learn much about the eating habits of the population. In her sincere desire to improve the meals, she never stopped to build her support networks. She left two months later, driven out by angry parents and teachers. At first, she was resentful and self-righteous; after all, didn't she have the best interests of the children at heart? It took several years for her to admit that time spent building good relationships with the staff could have created a working partnership, a partnership that would have had lasting, positive effects.

Sometimes, all you need to do to overcome a barrier or boundary is to acknowledge its importance. For example, you can tell the public relations committee chairperson that you know it is her prerogative to contact the media and that it is important that all media contacts go through her office. Say that you know the intention is to improve the quality of the contacts to the media. In that context, you can offer her your list of names. This kind of contact work is usually much more successful than sending out your own press releases beforehand and then having to apologize for preempting someone else's function.

On the other hand, sometimes you need to break some rules in order to function. In some institutions it is actually easier to apologize than to ask for permission ahead of time. Network builders must remember that networks take a long time to build and can be quite fragile. Doing the best you can, within the limits of common sense, to build a sense of community and trust is important in any situation where you are tempted to push ahead. Taking risks and getting things done does not have to be at the cost of damaging relationships with people who disagree with your methods.

There are no formulas to dealing with institutional boundaries. What is important is how the people involved feel they are treated. You do not have to acquiesce to every demand to stay off someone's turf, but you can acknowledge her feelings and the work that went into defining that turf in the first place.

Document Your Successes

Documentation is useful for building credibility with your superiors, for creating a history that credits the right people for their contributions, and for tracking contributions so that you can make and retrace connections. For example, you might have lost track of an important contributor and want to find the person who first told you about him.

The easiest aspects of network building to document are information products, such as mailing lists and directories. The hardest aspects are the informal meetings and connections, even though they are the most valuable. A former college community affairs director says that most of the work she did for the institution was invisible to her colleagues, which led to all kinds of resentment. For example, although her job description required her to be out in the public talking with community and business leaders, teachers and other staff members were angry because she seemed to spend all her time going to lunches and conferences. She knew, because she was an excellent network builder, that she needed to attend other people's events to build the kind of support the school needed. Unfortunately, she was better at building rapport with people outside her college than with those within. Part of the reason she was eventually fired was because she was never able to prove to her supervisor that her meetings were working.

This brings up the importance of using network building as a tool for accomplishing the named goals of the organization, rather than letting yourself become addicted to the process itself. To prove to your colleagues and supervisors that what you are doing works, you need more than a list of the phone calls you made or the conferences you attended. Successful network-building documentation includes these features:

1. A description of the goal, using the vocabulary of the institution. If the goal is a personal one, it should fit into the goals of your supervisors. Otherwise, it is not likely to be credible to them.

2. Several examples of measurable effects that reaching the goal would have on your institution and the staff.

3. Several examples of measurable effects you have been able to accomplish and how network building helped you achieve those goals.

The Network Workshop

A formal sharing of information about network building can be as easy as a brief talk during a staff luncheon or as complicated as a full-blown staff retreat. Remember, however, that actions speak louder than words. If your principal asks you to talk about network building with your fellow staff members, ask her to schedule the first five or ten minutes of each staff meeting as network-building time, when individuals can volunteer problems or resources they would like to share. Your presentation will have more meaning if it introduces some real, measurable change in the way your school operates.

What if you have the opportunity to conduct a longer training program for your peers or other members of your school community? The model for a successful network workshop has one main goal: to allow participants to exchange information. You do this by giving participants permission to talk with each other and by encouraging them to practice communication skills by working on what matters to each of them. Many workshops on communication fail because the participants never have the opportunity to communicate with each other—these workshops offer too much theory and not enough practice.

Two other important features characterize the successful network-building workshop. First, the exercises reflect reality and, second, participants have the opportunity to work on what is important to them. The object of the workshop is not building a consensus or a team. Consensus building and team building are important aspects of communication work; they complement both each other and network building. But they are not the same thing. Consensus building and team building are processes that focus on the group's shared ideas and concerns. Network building focuses on the relationships among individuals.

This difference might seem academic, but it exemplifies why networks are flexible, self-renewing, non-hierarchial, diverse, and fluid, as compared to most other forms of human organization. The most focused network is more dependent on the actions of each individual participant than is the most informal structured organization. The person who builds working relationships with others does it everywhere, not just among the members of the professional team. If the participants in your workshop start with what is important to them, they will be motivated to take the time and energy to build those relationships; the payoff is immediate and personal. Don't worry about consensus and teamwork during a network workshop. The common concerns come together quickly, often to the surprise of those who think it takes much more structure for people to be able to get things done.

Tips for a Successful Workshop

Appendix A contains detailed information on how to plan and run a networking workshop. Here are some tips to make your workshop more successful.

1.   Practice with a safe group.

If you are going to do a formal program for other staff members or as part of a professional training, practice first on a group of friends. Encourage them to give you feedback about your style. A good number to start with is 8 to 12 people.

2.   Let each individual work on her own problem.

The simplest way to start is to ask someone to offer a problem and then let the group suggest contacts or give advice. If no one volunteers, bring your own problem or problems to work on. It is rare when someone comes up with a problem about which no one can offer suggestions or information.

3.   Allow everyone to speak.

Make sure no individual dominates the conversation. In some structured network meetings each person has 30 seconds to state one problem or resource. Everyone takes notes, and then the floor is open for suggestions. In small groups, it is important that each person be heard by everyone. In larger groups, each person should be able to have several one-on-one conversations with other participants.

Remind participants that the heart of network building is the contact process. Ask them to keep track of suggestions, and encourage them to talk afterward about what they need to do. This kind of exercise can generate a lot of productive communication in the teachers' lounge.

4.   Get them laughing.

Humor is the best teacher. Serious subjects and heartfelt concerns are part of every network meeting, but so are laughter and goodwill. Good humor is one of the most successful tools for relaxing adult learners and allowing them to listen and to change new information into new behavior.[5]

Never make jokes at the expense of any participant, unless you are absolutely sure the person enjoys this kind of public kidding.

Also avoid making jokes about individuals who are not present at the meeting or about individuals who represent groups or organizations in your school community—word gets around, and you might never know how your words are being distorted.

When You Meet Resistance

Not everyone in your school will consider your efforts to be in their best interests or in the best interests of your school. A school media specialist who is part of a successful network-based team says her success stems from the excellent working relationships she already had with her co-workers. Without those close relationships, she doubts she would be as successful. And, she admits, some of her colleagues are not as supportive as they might be.

You can accomplish anything as long as your superiors and colleagues are supportive, particularly the principal, who is the key person in setting the tone of the school. But what if that support is not readily given? Do the best you can. Use your own networks well, but don't turn networking into a religion or start trying to convert others.

Dealing with Critical Feedback

Each piece of critical feedback can provide you with useful information about your efforts. Sometimes critics will provide you with valid feedback about your networking style that shows areas where you might need to change. Other times, the resistance has nothing to do with you or your network building; it may stem from issues people have with your supervisor or with the person who previously was in your position. And some people may feel personally or professionally threatened by your efforts to reach out. Some of the most common complaints about network building and network builders include:

1. They give me too much information that is not relevant to my own efforts.

2. It takes up too much of my time and resources with little immediate payoff.

3. The network builder is more interested in communicating new ideas than following through with what he or she has already started.

4. I feel as if I am being pushed to share sensitive information.

5. They want something for nothing.

6. I am expected to instantly trust a stranger with my best contacts.

7. I keep getting calls from jobhunters who want me to counsel them for free.

8. The network builder keeps sending me salespeople who are trying to sell me something I don't want.

9. Every time I ask the network builder a question, I get 10 phone numbers I am supposed to call. And those 10 people each have 10 more numbers!

10. I resent the network builder's effort to "fix" me.

11. It is a new part of my job description, but I am not being paid for the extra work.

12. It doesn't work.

13. I did a bunch of research for another group, and now I feel as if I were exploited—nothing happened.

14. I trusted someone and was betrayed.

People Have the Right To Say "No Thank You"

Remember that everyone has the right to say no to your requests for information or offers of assistance. Some people whom you would like to have as part of one of your active networks might never be more than first-name acquaintances. Perhaps they are overwhelmed by the demands of their personal or professional lives. Perhaps they have set clear boundaries about who they will and won't support.

In *Teacher as Servant* (New York: Paulist Press, 1979), author Robert Greenleaf makes the case for those who set clear limits on what they will and won't do in the community. His main role model, a professor who regards his family, his classes, and his supervised student group as his only interests, seems to have been created in response to those community activists who neglect their families and their professional duties by stretching themselves over too many meetings and organizations. Perhaps someone is saying no because they feel they are already committed to the hilt.

The same people who tell you no may actually be pleased with what you are doing and refer others to you.

Preventing Problems

Considering what can go wrong when human beings try to communicate with each other, it is amazing the world runs as smoothly as it does. Below is a checklist of some common-sense approaches to preventing problems in your network-building attempts. They can also help you address the question of "what now" when things go wrong.

1. Make few promises, and keep the ones you make.

2. Give only one or two connections to people whom you don't know well, and then get feedback from both them and the other parties.

3. If something is important, follow through yourself.

4. Assume that personal chemistry can create problems between intelligent and nice people, even those with whom you have never had a problem.

5. Document what you are doing if it is related to your school or profession. Create a legal trail, if necessary, by making notes after meetings and following up verbal agreements with brief written memos.

6. Use your network building to serve others, rather than to build your own empire. Try to strengthen existing efforts whenever possible, rather than to reinvent the wheel or the community drug program or the school-business partnership that 20 other groups are running.

7. Avoid what psychologists call "triangulation." If two people are having a problem, avoid carrying tales back and forth between them.

When Things Go Wrong

1. Reserve judgment until you have heard everyone's story.

2. Offer to mediate or to find a mediator, but don't engage in gossip. If the parties want to trade blame instead of solving

the problem and moving on to something else, disengage yourself from their battle.

3. Take responsibility for whatever part you might have had in a problem, but don't put energy into blaming other people. Fix the problem, not the blame.

4. Take other people's concerns seriously, but stay good-humored and friendly, even when others become upset or hysterical.

5. Keep asking "What could I have done differently?" until you get an answer that you can use, and thank people for their feedback.

6. Expect that you and your fellow network participants are not perfect. Remember to forgive other people and yourself when things go awry.

In a community of network builders, there is a feeling of safety and resourcefulness among most of the participants. There are few "stars," but many effective communicators. As a benefit, people are more willing to take chances, because they know there are others they can rely on for help. Diversity is promoted and personal initiative is rewarded. Partnerships are not mandated, but grow out of the culture of the community. If you do your job well, you may never get credit for your work, because the network building will seem to have generated spontaneously from a dozen sources.

Notes

1. *Servant Leadership* (New York: Paulist Press, 1977) by Robert K. Greenleaf is the classic management text on transforming organizations by personal example. A companion book, *Teacher as Servant* (New York: Paulist Press, 1979) is a well-written didactic novel about an unusual experiment in a college that fosters network building and community participation. As with many classics about building support networks, the word *network* is never mentioned. See Appendix C for more information.

2. Beth Wheeler Fox has created a terrific handbook for creating networks in *The Dynamic Community Library* (Chicago: American Library Association, 1988). Her chapter on finding and keeping good volunteers emphasizes the need to promote the accomplishments of volunteers.

3. An interesting text to skim on the purposes and effects of gossip and rumor in institutions and society is aptly named *Rumor and Gossip: The Social Psychology of Hearsay* (New York: Elsevier, 1976), by Ralph L. Rosnow and

Gary Alan Fine. See Appendix C for more information.

4. Other characteristics included a safe and supportive environment, strong instructional leadership, high expectations, and monitoring and feedback of student progress. For more information about the Effective Schools Program and how it is transforming schools with mostly Native American students throughout the United States, write to the Bureau of Indian Affairs/Minneapolis Area Office, 15 S. Fifth Street, Minneapolis, MN 55402.

5. Several books on personal growth and development in Appendix C advocate the use of humor as a way to relieve stress and encourage learning.

———— 10 ————

Using Networks To Cope with Stress and Crises

Could your personal or professional support network literally save your life? In their landmark book *The Healing Web: Social Networks and Human Survival* (Hanover, NH: University Press of New England, 1986), authors Marc Pilisuk and Susan Hillier Parks demonstrate that the biological and social bonds of human community not only buffer the spirit from the traumas of life, but they also actually protect the physical body from harm. A 1990 proclamation from the American Institute for Preventative Medicine listed 10 ways to prevent disease and live a longer, healthier life; developing a social support network was ranked in importance with diet, exercise, and using seatbelts.[1]

For people in the helping professions, including teachers, librarians, social workers, and psychologists, service is the norm and their own needs are sometimes neglected. When it comes to networking, caring professionals are likely to think about being useful to other people while neglecting to ask for something for themselves in return. Sometimes it takes a major personal or professional crisis to push a self-reliant person into the networking mode. Support networks can play a major role in helping you cope with both personal and institutional stress and crises.

Internal Stress: Personal Crises and Needs

Remember, learning to network means learning to ask for help. If you are practicing building relationships with other individuals and the projects they represent, you have the opportunity to tap into the almost infinite resources of your many networks. All you need to do is ask.

In a network workshop at a master reading class at the University of Northern Colorado in 1990, class members were asked to make a list of their needs. They wrote down the kinds of everyday things that all adults need at some time or other: help with fixing a car, a job for a teenage son, time to clean the house. They were stunned to discover that someone else in the room had a suggestion for almost every problem mentioned, including the mysterious car ailment that several mechanics had been unable to solve. What was even more surprising was how eagerly the members of the class helped solve each other's problems.

Later the professor commented that he had rarely seen the people in his class so talkative. This class had been meeting for several weeks, and the students were, for the most part, seasoned teaching professionals. Yet none of the participants had thought to take advantage of the proximity of other resourceful adults to ask for assistance. The class members had been so intent on the content of the class that they had neglected to pay attention to the opportunity to build working relationships with each other.

These are some of the requests for assistance that came out of one networking session with a group of rural librarians and educators.

1. A place to buy eyeglasses (the request came from someone who had just moved to the area from out of state)

2. Information to exchange with someone who was planting a vineyard

3. How to help a child adjust to having to wear braces

4. Information on buying computers for the school

5. Inexpensive vacation ideas for farm families

6. Information about local community organizations that might want to sponsor school projects

7. Specialists who could come to class to give good talks on wild animals that live in the region

8. How to manage stress (this one appeared in some form or other on almost everyone's list)

9. More time (also appeared on everyone's list)

10. Time for reading (this and "time for filing" seem to be most commonly requested among school media specialists)

11. Ideas for menus that are inexpensive, healthy, tasty, can be made ahead or frozen, and can be made by a child or unhandy spouse

12. Ways to help one's own children resolve issues concerning after-school activities (this from a teacher who said she had trouble guiding and supporting her own children because of her emotional involvement)

13. How to handle twins

Think of your own current list of needs. Who could you ask for help? In almost all workshops with professionals, the "needs" lists for both male and female participants are divided evenly between personal and job-related requests. This is not true just of teachers and school librarians, but of other working adults as well. One trainer reported that after she had presented a major program on information and communication techniques for a large corporation, the first question from the floor was, "How do I get my husband to take out the garbage?"

Some school professionals seem to think there is something wrong with asking other staff people for help with personal problems. During network-building workshops, at least one of the participants usually protests that it is not appropriate to bring domestic problems to work. However, there is a big difference between someone whose life is a continuous soap opera and who seems to receive some pleasure from the never-ending disasters and someone who is actively seeking solutions to real problems. Experienced network builders report that their networks literally become their safety nets. What are some of the specific ways network building can help during a personal crisis?

1. You have people you can turn to in case of unexpected changes or emergencies.

For example, because you know your next door neighbor well and have her work phone number, you can call her to look after your pets when you are unexpectedly called out of town.

2. Connections with those in other fields can mean free or inexpensive advice or help when you have a personal need.

One private school teacher tells about a financial crisis that prevented his school from giving raises, thereby causing several excellent teachers to consider leaving because of personal budget crises. Parents who owned retail stores or offered professional services gave substantial discounts to the teachers. A car dealership owner was able to convince one teacher to stay by offering him an incredible deal on a new car!

3. A diverse network within the school community can be used as a reality check during a community emergency.

During a threatened teachers' strike, two middle school teachers received their information differently. One, a devoted teacher with average network-building skills, complained that her only sources of information were the union hotline and the newspapers. The other, a superb network builder, was going out for drinks and meals with other teachers, principals, and school employees. She made sure that her contacts on the "other side" knew that she wanted to keep in touch with them to compare ideas, not to argue or accuse. Guess which teacher had the most accurate information and the best professional support?

An elementary school teacher reports that one of the main reasons she volunteers to serve on various "thinktank" committees and citizen programs is to "stick her nose into what is going on." Even though she does not think of herself as a "political" person, she has met many of the movers and shakers in the educational establishment in her state; these connections have helped her make career decisions.

Here are a few network building techniques to consider the next time you are hit with a personal crisis at home or school.

1. Talk it over with another person.

Sometimes talking something over with someone else does not add more significant data to help solve the problem. However, stress is often relieved because of the magic of "talking it out." In one study conducted on stress in school teachers, "talking to a friend," using "a support system," and "blowing off steam" were all coping techniques teachers used to deal with job stress. This has been verified in other studies.[2]

If you do not want instant advice about what to do about the problem, tell the other person up front you want to use them as a sounding board. Cultivate these kinds of good listeners in your personal network.

2. Find someone who has gone through the same thing.

One of the precepts of network building is that someone has built the gadget that you need or has already researched the problem and found solutions. In personal crisis management, it is good to assume that many people in your personal network have already dealt with the same issue or know someone who has.

A group of teachers from an elementary school in a small city were surveyed about what kinds of inservice communication programs would help them most in their work. Out of 22 teachers, all but one wrote down almost identical requests for assistance in dealing with conflict with other teachers. More than half of the group specifically mentioned that they wanted to learn how to talk with colleagues about disagreements arising from differences of opinion about classroom procedure and from personality differences. When the results of the survey were revealed to the group, several people expressed surprise that their fellow teachers had the same concerns and problems they did.

3. Anticipate problems.

The director of a major consumer "helpline" program says many of the horror stories she hears about shady deals, faulty products, and poor service arise because the alleged victim never asked for a second opinion before signing a contract or making a payment. A private detective who specializes in business and investment fraud reports that doctors, lawyers, teachers and other degreed professionals are considered "easy marks" for financial scams because they are less likely to ask questions; pretending to understand the details of a questionable investment is more important to them than revealing their ignorance.

If you cultivate a network of specialists in areas such as car repair, finance (your banker is a good place to start), law, home mortgages, medicine (medical librarians report that more and more reference questions are coming from patients who want to do some of their own research), and insurance (find an agent who will give you service, not just sell you a policy and disappear), you are less likely to be helpless when the inevitable mistakes happen. The trick is to use your connections before problems develop. Devout network builders treat the energy they spend checking and double-checking situations and people like a good insurance policy. They do not become disappointed or consider it a waste of time when their network participants report that "everything is fine."

Some school media specialists are reluctant to seek another person for advice, preferring to look up the information in a book or online computer database. They may call a person on behalf of a student or patron, but will sometimes hesitate to call an expert on behalf of themselves. The problem with this approach, as pointed out elsewhere, is that written information is often out-of-date. Nothing can substitute for talking to an expert who is current in the field.

External Stress: Professional and Institutional Crises

An elementary school principal in a small town in the West described one week in his professional career. First, a group of sixth-grade girls from his school was implicated in a prostitution ring being run out of a nearby motel. Then one of the younger students was the only eyewitness to a murder. To add to his stress, the boy's name was accidentally released by the local newspaper. Finally, a younger student begged a teacher to help protect his mother and siblings from his violent father. The authorities were notified, and social workers, police, and school personnel were working together to change what had escalated into a dangerous situation.

Although it was not typical, this week exemplified what the principal felt many school professionals faced on a regular basis. "Is it any wonder," he asked, "that I jumped a foot that week whenever a staff member came into my office for the simplest request?" Institutional crises like these fall into several categories.

The "Ostrich" Crisis

The "ostrich" disaster is the crisis that everyone knew was in the making but hoped would go away if no one said anything about it or acknowledged its presence.

A high school coach who left the profession after 20 years tells about his principal, who did not want district officials to know that gangs had gained a foothold in his building. He ordered that gang graffiti be cleaned off the walls between classes, but he never reported the incidents and denied there was a problem. Consequently, the school administration officials reported to law enforcement agencies that there was no problem. Now the gangs have escalated beyond control.

A community organizer in New Jersey was unable to distribute a free, effective video series on drug prevention in target counties in his state because many principals said, "We have no drug problem." This was in the early 1980s. He could not convince these administrators that even if there were no drugs being used in their schools, they could use the videos as a kind of preventive medicine.

A specialist in business-school partnerships who has worked in the Pacific Northwest says that this tendency of school administrators to try to present a perfect picture of their schools is not uncommon. But it can sabotage partnerships with business, because the two partners have different agendas. Businesses tend to have a bottom line, which ideally measures success and learns from failure. Conversely, the political structure of the public school system, she says, encourages a mentality that denies failure. Administrative denial can also be a symptom of administrative burnout.

Network building in ostrich crises might mean preparing for the inevitable. For example, many teachers educated themselves on issues like drugs and teenage pregnancy before doing so became an official policy of their institutions. This meant taking the time to seek out experts in these issues outside of their own professions. Successful network building over the long term can create the trust needed to fight the ostrich syndrome, but for most school community members, network building happens after the fact.

Managing the Ostrich Crisis

A skilled network builder can turn a crisis into an opportunity.

In one midwestern city in the "Rust Belt," the demise of the local automobile plant had been predicted for decades. There was well-publicized hostility between the union and local school officials over the issue of persuading children to stay in school as long as possible to finish their educations and train for careers outside of the automotive industry. Further, the antagonism between the union and local business owners had long been part of the city's culture.

The local superintendent of schools was able to use a potentially sticky situation to build bridges between the warring factions. A group of business people was accustomed to addressing school classes on business and management practices. Union officials approached the school district and demanded to review the information the business owners and managers were presenting about union negotiation. They seemed convinced that the information being presented was anti-union. Their anger was not unanticipated by the school administration. The superintendent saw an opportunity for some coalition building and suggested that the union officials not only review the materials, but also work with the business people to prepare and present the materials.

The union officials were surprised at how little of the material they did not like, and, after some hesitancy, they agreed to the plan. The partnership has been a success for several years and, according to the superintendent, is one of the few places in the region that you can see union officials and management sitting at the same table and smiling.

The "Cyclical" Crisis

Another kind of crisis is the "cyclical" crisis of economic downturns, legislative action, and school bond issues. In this kind of crisis, the problems have some public recognition and even a recognizable deadline. In most school communities, there is plenty of time to prepare; the question is, what kind of preparation and when does it begin?

School bond issues are the most crucial crises for most school districts and the best example of the mismanaged cyclical crisis. According to *Public Relations, Promotions, and Fund-Raising for Athletics and Physical Education Programs* (New York: John Wiley & Sons, 1977), the main reason that school bond issues fail is because parents and other members of the voting public feel left out of the process. Building the appropriate networks becomes even more challenging when you consider that voters with school-age children have become a minority in many school districts. Obviously, the school district that hopes to succeed at capturing an election cannot start a few weeks before election day or rely only on the support of parents. A slick public relations campaign might even alienate voters, particularly older citizens who feel as if they have paid their dues and do not feel they can afford the higher property taxes that accompany a rise in the mill rate.

In a real sense, a school bond election is a litmus test of what the paying customers of the school district think of the product they have been sold the previous years. Businesses are used to having to please their customers with every transaction or risk losing them. However, the average public school district employee is not used to the kind of interactive relationship inherent in business between the one who pays and the one who receives the money.

Similarly, if media representatives perceive a policy of secrecy and evasiveness on the part of a school district administration, an onslaught of newsletters and press releases before a school bond election is not going to win them over. The community affairs director of a major television station with several years of experience with school issues says his biggest problem with school boards is their unwillingness to answer questions about their activities. Consequently, the press thinks they are "hiding something," and the hostilities begin. The solution is more honesty, he says, on the part of both the schools and the press.

Teachers and school media specialists who have had business experience before or during their school careers have commented on the difference "selling" made in their school careers. One school librarian said that her success in increasing circulation in her library came from years of having to make a living from straight commissions. She felt she was more service-oriented than some of her colleagues and more aware of the importance of documenting her successes to supervisors, patrons, and the public. Another teacher said that selling taught her to ask people what they wanted; it even extended to her offering her students choices about reading materials and asking them what they wanted to know.

Business has learned that customer service cannot be something that is added on as an afterthought. It starts with how people are treated as they come in the front door and extends to the way problems and complaints are resolved. Consumers in every field are demanding better service, and the school systems are no exception.

If your school district won its last bond election, did you thank the members of your school community and use the success as an opportunity to build new alliances? Is an election coming up? Now is the time to ask questions and find out what the various participants of your networks are saying about your school. Use that information to decide what people need to know to vote yes. Remember that bad news is good information, and negative feedback should be welcomed.

If the election is imminent, you can still try to meet with key community leaders from both supportive and nonsupportive groups and find out what it would take to get their yes votes. If a loss seems inevitable or has already occurred, the school district can use the vote to motivate the community to participate in making changes in the school system. Ask business leaders for advice on restructuring budgets and supporting special programs. Beef up your volunteer recruitment programs. Ask for a public postmortem and make sure the community knows that your school is going to use this defeat as an opportunity to learn. Stay positive about the members of community who said no; they are not necessarily "antischool," just dissatisfied or feeling uninvolved.

The Crisis Management Network

Every school building and school district should have a crisis plan to cover the unexpected. This means having:

1. A core team of personnel, representing every part of the school community, who prepare themselves and other members of the school for crisis

2. A crisis policy manual or written directions to cover issues such as the line of command, communicating with key groups such as parents, and talking to the media

3. Crisis training in emergency first aid, building evacuation, and cooperating with government and law enforcement officials

4. A designated rumor-control person or office to give out accurate information to parents and other concerned citizens

5. Training or support in post-crisis trauma and management, particularly as it applies to children and staff

Some crises, like natural disasters and weather emergencies, have been anticipated by government officials, and the mechanisms for dealing with them are in place. However, school personnel should check to make sure information is current and complete. For example, are the phone numbers for the media accurate? Do new employees know what they need to do? When was the last time employees were checked on CPR? Is there a new policy at local hospitals that would affect where injured students might be taken in a crisis? Is parent or guardian contact information up to date? One television and radio reporter advises school

160

personnel to make sure their Rolodex of emergency numbers is current and complete, with the correct names, addresses, and titles of key people.

What about the crises not covered by Civil Defense handouts or the local emergency planning board? Here are three school-related crises that occurred recently in one community. Would your school be prepared to handle them? Some were straightforward events; others were made worse by poor communications and lack of trust.

1. The school board treasurer was caught stealing money from the treasury.

2. A dangerous individual was threatening students at neighborhood schools. The police were notified, but parents were not. The doors at one elementary school were locked to keep the intruder out. A parent, arriving late one morning with her child, found the school doors locked and discovered the cause. She publicly berated school personnel for violating fire laws and not telling her that her child might be in danger.

3. A teacher was accused of sexually molesting students. Parents asserted that they had been trying to report this man for years, but were hushed up by school officials. In the middle of the televised trial, the names of several of the molested students were accidentally flashed on the screen.

A crisis network is an insurance network that, with luck, you will never have to use. In terms of structure, a formal network organization that keeps up with the changing information inside and outside the school building or district is probably the most appropriate model.

When Not To Network

Believe it or not, there are times when you shouldn't try to build or use a support network. The process of exchanging information is not a panacea, nor is it an end in itself.

Covert Networks and Political Backrooms

The worst application of school networks is using connections to sabotage or undercut honest communication and fair practices among teachers, students, and administrators. Everyone is familiar with examples of such misconduct, from the parent who uses her contacts on the school board to affect a child's grade, to activists who use their access to the media to air disputes without trying to work them out beforehand, to people who use their influences to make sure a job goes to a friend or relative. In such cases, people use the process of communication to avoid dealing with the people involved or to gain undeserved power in a situation. Needless to say, this kind of power brokering is not what this book is about.

Personal and Professional Burnout Indicators

The purpose of network building is to enhance your work and your personal life, not to replace them. Following are some indications that you need to examine your behavior and perhaps declare a network-building hiatus:

1. You are using meetings, phone calls, and postcards as an excuse to not get your primary work done, be it teaching, parenting, or running the school.

2. You turn every personal conversation into a business meeting.

3. You are losing your sense of humor and your sense of perspective.

4. You feel angry when people say "no thank you" to your attempts to help them.

5. You are spending more and more money on elaborate filing systems, but your pile of filing is not getting any smaller.

6. Network building has become a chore.

7. You feel compulsive about knowing information first.

8. All of your relationships are working relationships, and everyone you know has assignments from you to fulfill.

Any of these behaviors and feelings is a sign that you need to take a break.

When You Are the Newcomer

Sometimes network building can been seen by others as threatening behavior, particularly in cross-cultural situations where you are not familiar with other languages and mores. In these cases, go slowly. In a tightly knit community where you are perceived as an outsider, nothing but the passage of time will convince the members of the community that you are someone worthy of their trust and confidence. In some situations, you may always be the outsider, and nothing you do will break down the barriers. In those situations, it is useless to feel resentful, and overt action might be counterproductive.

What can you do if you find yourself in such an isolated situation? Keep your long-distance relationships alive with letters and phone calls; intellectual and emotional community does not require proximity to succeed. If you are in one of those rare situations where you cannot easily communicate with your support network, keep a journal of your thoughts and the events in your life. You can see your role as a listener and a learner, rather than the one who builds relationships or initiates actions. The respect you show for other people in the community can build relationships, even though they might not be the kind you are accustomed to.

Creating a Vacuum So Others Can Network

The best reason to stop trying to build networks is so other people can. Even the best-intentioned and sensitive network builder can undermine the independence and creativity of the people she serves by doing her job too well. Your network is getting stagnant if:

1. Your informal network of friendly and helpful people is slowly turning into a clique of old-timers who delight in passing verdicts on new ideas and new people

2. You and other established participants in your network demand and get special privileges

3. It gets tougher every year to become a new participant in your networks, and recruiting is becoming a major issue

4. New networks are forming specifically to oppose the ideas and values of your established network

5. The average age of your network participants is going up, while members of other networks are relatively younger

6. Your network is made up of the same faces

Perhaps you need to be talking with some new people or building relationships with newcomers to your school or community. Also, perhaps your informal alliances have matured into the very kind of bureaucracies you were attempting to circumvent in the first place. As he neared retirement, community organizer Saul Alinksy began to receive calls from people who wanted him to help them deal with "bullies" and the "establishment" in neighborhoods he had worked in years before. He discovered in more than one case that the "bullies" were people he himself had helped organize when they were the disenfranchised. Changing the players in the power structure was not enough.

Smugness is a subtle and addictive vice. You might be surprised to find yourself being criticized by a new generation of community builders. The antidote is fresh faces, fresh ideas, and a sabbatical from your role as "professional networker."

Notes

1. *Rocky Mountain News*, December 30, 1990, p. 4.
2. Jeanine Wyly and Susan Frusher, "Stressors and Coping Strategies of Teachers," *Rural Educator*, Vol. 2, No. 2: 29–31.

11

The Next Step

It starts with a smile and a decision to share it:

Who will be the next person with whom you exchange a laugh, a friendly greeting, a small act of goodwill, or a tip on why not to eat the mashed potatoes in the cafeteria?

Who will be the next colleague you decide to forgive for a careless slight five years ago?

Who will be the next member of your school staff you decide to praise with genuine enthusiasm?

Who will be the next professional you call for help?

Who will be the next couple you write with good news about their child's progress or a note about something amusing she said in your class?

Who will be the next old friend you call to catch up with on your current professional concerns?

Who will be the next neighbor whom you poll about his opinion of your school?

It starts with curiosity about the people and projects in your community:

What are the parents of your students really like, outside of their roles as parents?

What are the teachers of your students really like, outside of their roles as teachers?

If you talk to someone you perceive as your enemy, could

you learn something from him or her?

If you spend less time in meetings talking with people whose roles in the school and community are identical to yours and more time in your school and community talking with people who have roles different from yours, what will you discover about your role? What will you discover about their roles?

What can the public librarian in another school's neighborhood teach you about your school?

What can both the large and the small businesses in the neighborhood donate to help your school make do with less money?

What advice and financial expertise can local business owners share with the school's budget committee?

The Ultimate School Networking Fantasy

1. Conflict resolution, negotiation, public speaking, stress management, and community relations are an important part of every teacher's training. Along the same lines, all of the best, most interesting, most enjoyable, and most effective trainers in business and industry are invited to share their wisdom about personal and professional development with teachers and other staff members.

2. Every teacher in every school has his or her own telephone, with a direct line and an answering machine. If that is not possible, each school has a voice mail system with a private number for every staff member, including the principal and the assistant janitor.

3. Every staff member of every school system has his or her own business cards, including the custodial staff, the bus drivers, the dieticians, and the clerical staff. Each card includes the name of the school, the school mission statement, and the private number of the staff member.

4. Every staff member of every school system has at least one day each month to go into the community and meet with people, in both formal and informal settings. This includes, but is not limited to, trips to the following organizations (with a few suggested individuals to visit):

Local, state, and federal government offices (those of both appointed and elected officials)

Businesses of all sizes (a self-employed artist, the CEO of a Fortune 500 business)

Nonprofit organizations (United Way employees, radical social change activists)

Community and recreation centers (swimming coaches, immigration counselors)

Public libraries (branch and main building staffers, besides the children's librarian)

Other schools, including public, private, religious, and trade (private school principals, trade school trainers)

Universities and colleges (department heads outside the teaching college, support personnel)

Senior centers, hospices, and nursing homes (both residents and staff members)

Hospitals, clinics, and community health centers (the director of marketing, the medical staff)

Shelters for the homeless and street clinics for teenage runaways (both residents and staff)

Farms and ranches (migrant workers, farm family members)

Law enforcement agencies (police officers, district attorneys)

Day care centers and child care facilities (staff and children)

Rallies, public forums, community events, and press conferences (community activists, visiting dignitaries)

The offices of the media, including print and electronic (reporters, editors, technicians)

Veterans' organizations and political parties (party activists, elderly war veterans)

Religious and cultural institutions (ministers, musicians)

The office of the superintendent of schools (the superintendent, the superintendent's secretary)

Family adults at home and at work (grandparents, live-in "friends" of single parents)

5. Every staff member is encouraged and supported to actively seek out and welcome parental visits at any time. Adults visiting the school building are treated like favorite customers of a well-run retail store, regardless of how they are dressed or their position in the community.

6. Every school staff member has the opportunity and the budget to attend luncheon meetings of local business, professional, and service groups.

7. All of those factions who might be involved in negotiating a contract between a school system and a particular group of school employees create an active networking organization.

Members include school board members, the staff of the office of the superintendent, union officials, the officers of professional associations, school staff, students, parents, community group leaders, government officials, and members of the state legislature. Anyone can participate.

The organization has two purposes: first, to conduct ongoing training programs on negotiation for any interested network participants, but particularly for individuals who might be involved in a contract negotiation at a future date; second, to create a series of friendly networking events, including picnics and community suppers, so that participants get to know each other without the pressures of contract deadlines, television cameras, and angry special interest groups.

8. Finally, everyone in the school community treats each other and each member of the greater community with the same respect, good humor, and compassion that they desire for themselves.

You have tremendous power to improve our schools and our communities, and it starts with taking a few minutes to talk with an expert, visit a neighbor, or write a short letter.

It starts with a handshake, a shared joke, a common concern.

It starts with a smile.

Appendix A

How To Run a Networking Workshop

The Physical Environment

A workshop on building networks works best if the setting allows participants to get up and move around during and after the program. This means movable chairs and tables, a multiple-table conference setting with groups of chairs around each table, or movable student chairs with built-in desktops.

If these configurations are not possible, request an unstructured placement of furniture, such as a circle of chairs; an informal grouping of chairs, pillows, and couches in a teachers' lounge; or even a living room in a private home. Since the purpose of the workshop is to entice participants into talking with each other, it is more important that they be facing each other than looking at the workshop facilitator.

This kind of program can also work in a large conference room with no chairs. It has been conducted for several hundred librarians at one time at state and national conventions in large rooms, with enough seating for only a few dozen participants. The programs go quickly, and few people complain of tired feet.

Good handouts and a board to write out information are useful tools, but once the members of the audience have the idea that they can solve problems by talking to each other, you become more and more superfluous to the process. You can even leave for several minutes, and no one will notice you are gone.

Check out adjoining rooms and hallways and find out before the program starts if it will be permissible for some of the exercises to overflow into other space. You will need to warn the people in charge that a networking workshop is a noisy affair. This surprises conference and program organizers who assume that *workshop* is a euphemism for *lecture*. The amount of noise that even a small group of individuals can generate is astounding. If noise becomes a problem, you can revert to written exercises, but spoken interaction is preferable.

Coping with an Auditorium

The least useful environment is an auditorium or classroom with fixed seats. If you find yourself forced into conducting a program in such a structured and formal environment, modify the exercises to accommodate the barriers. First, entice, cajole, threaten, or bribe participants to sit close to the front. If there are empty seats close to the front and people in the rear are having trouble hearing, politely suggest that they move. Then forgo the podium and move as close as possible to the edge of the stage, or even into the aisle.

Since workshop participants will be eager to record information, writing surfaces of some kind are useful. Many school auditoriums have flip-down desks, but these can make some adult audience members feel mildly claustrophobic.

Encourage participants to sit next to other people in the audience so that they will have a partner to talk with during the program. With groups of less than 50, you can sometimes delay the program for a few minutes by asking all of the participants to stand up and then sit next to someone they don't know or, at the very least, someone they don't know very well. Also, you can shorten the formal part of the program so that members of the audience can stick around and talk with each other in the aisles and at the front of the auditorium.

Coping with Bad Acoustics

Acoustics can be crucial to the success of the presentation. Dozens of simultaneous conversations can create nerve-racking chaos in a high-ceiling hall with no acoustical material in the floor, walls, or ceiling. Such a facility also is a challenge for the workshop leader, who, even with an adequate public address system, must scream to be heard.

Try to check out the space you are being asked to occupy before the program. At the same time, test the microphone and speaker system. Try to get a portable microphone so you can move around and talk to audience members directly. If you can project your voice well, you can sometimes give up on the electronics and go with your unaided voice.

Using Helpers

In groups of over 100 people, you can ask for helpers to assist you. You might request one helper for every 20 to 25 participants and convene them for 15 to 30 minutes before the workshop. Present a short version of the program, then ask them to roam around the room during the real thing, looking for people who seem confused or who have not found a partner for the current exercise. It is helpful, but not necessary, to have helpers wear special badges or armbands.

Sometimes participants are overly concerned with doing an exercise the "right" way, instead of just doing it. The helpers' task is to encourage conversations, which might mean doing nothing but finding their own partners with whom to exchange ideas.

The Tools

Although some participants will want handouts (which are better to distribute *after* the program is over), visual aids can distract the audience members from the important work of the program, which is not necessarily listening to the facilitator obediently and looking at slides or overhead transparencies. When in doubt, limit yourself to the bare minimum of tools, so that you are not tempted to lecture about theory when your audience needs a chance to act.

At the end of this appendix is a handout to use in your programs. Please feel free to copy and adapt the information as you like, giving appropriate credit to ABC-CLIO and *Building Support Networks for Schools.*

The Exercises

Exercise One: Be Useful

The process of network building is so obvious that the more you talk about it, the more likely you are to confuse your audience. It is better to plunge your participants into the process as fast as possible, so they don't have time to think about why it won't work. Show them that it works and that it will work for them on their own terms.

The first exercise begins with a brief introduction. Tell the audience that they are going to practice networking, which is a skill they all already possess. Then announce that you are going to follow the five rules of good networking, the first of which is "Be Useful and Let Others Be Useful to You."

Tell the audience that, when you say "go," you want each person to locate a partner (if the seating is fixed, this choice has been made for them). To facilitate this process, suggest that each person raise a hand while looking and then lower his or her hand when a partner is found. The only other instruction is for each person to try to be useful to his or her partner and to allow the partner to be useful to him or her. Announce that they have five minutes to complete the exercise, and say "Go!"

Amidst some laughing and confusion, most participants quickly will find a partner and, with no other encouragement, settle down for a productive conversation. A small percentage of participants will want detailed instructions; kindly but firmly repeat that they are to "try to be useful to each other."

At the end of five minutes, ask participants to find another partner and to listen for the next instructions. This part rarely goes smoothly, which is a tribute to the success of the first exercise. Most of the partners will balk at finding someone new. There will be much scrambling to exchange contact information. Many will refuse to stop talking. And those who are willing to find a new partner will immediately begin talking and not wait for the next set of instructions. Rather than become upset, use the friendly defiance of the audience members as a way of demonstrating to them how easy it is to engage in useful and productive conversations, if they are given permission. Eventually the group will more or less settle down and wait for the next exercise. Don't be disturbed if some participants refuse to switch partners, or if they carry on conversations surreptitiously.

Exercise Two: Build Networks on Behalf of Others

It is very important to separate the pairs formed in the first exercise; otherwise, most of your audience will cheerfully talk with each other and ignore you through the rest of the program.

While you have their attention, ask your audience what happened during the first exercise. Did they discover any coincidences? Were there any surprises? Was anyone useful to anyone else? Sharing the successes and the interesting confluences of needs and offers can reinforce the individual successes and demonstrate that useful networking is not a fluke. For those people who had no more than a pleasant conversation, the practical experiences of some of the other participants might spark some ideas about what can happen.

At this point, depending on the amount of time available to you and the group, you can ask people to repeat the first exercise with their current partner. Remind them that they also can make connections on behalf of their first partner. Remind them, too, that even if they are strangers, they can trade business cards or take down the other person's address and phone number at the beginning of the conversation. Also, explain that network building is based on reciprocity and that both parties need to practice being useful to each other. This time, give the paired members more time to make their exchanges.

After this exercise, you can choose to repeat the process with new partners. If you instead continue with a new exercise, you should still have your participants switch partners before you go on.

Exercise Three: Identify "Needs" and "Offers"

During this part of the workshop, participants will need paper, pencil, and a place to write. Using the model in "The Five Rules of Networking" from Chapter 1, discuss with audience members their successes and failures so far in the context of the second rule.

Now that your audience is beginning to see how easy it might be to build networks, encourage them to plan for opportunity. A variation of this exercise can be included in the formal structure of faculty meetings, professional conferences, and other gatherings among school personnel.

Planning encourages both "givers" and "takers" to become more balanced in their approach to networking. It helps "givers" identify needs that others can fulfill, and "takers" are reminded of what they can do for others.

Ask each member of the audience to make two written lists. One list should contain "needs," which, in the broadest sense of the word, include personal and professional needs, wants, and desires. They can be practical or fanciful, short-term or long-term. In the same spirit, the second list contains "offers," both tangible and intangible; encourage the participants to write down many kinds of offers. Set a specific number of items in each list and a time deadline for finishing the lists; give the audience less time than they need so they don't have time to linger.

Lead a discussion with participants about what kinds of things they put on their list. Who found it hard to come up with "needs"; "offers"? What items appeared on many lists? What comments from the audience triggered (or are triggering) ideas for other participants? What items were unique to each list? What items tended to occur in both lists?

Ask participants to begin sharing ideas and solutions with their new partners. There is no right way or wrong way to do this; some partners will chuck the lists and just talk.

Exercise Four: Play the Wild Card

There are many variations on the workshop, but the main objectives are, first, to get people to talk to each other and, second, to get them to think about writing down what kinds of things they might transact in a network. This exercise demonstrates the amazing diversity of the networks individuals might inhabit and use without even thinking.

Describe some of the kinds of networks participants might use and the hundreds of connections they might make in the course of a year. Then ask participants to volunteer their most difficult requests. Require that the requests be specific and that participants be serious about finding a solution. When participants volunteer, ask them to stand and identify themselves to the group, if it is an audience where there is any chance that individuals might not know each other well and by sight. Ask them to state their need or want. If necessary, ask questions to clarify the need.

Now ask the audience to offer suggestions of contacts, advice, and connections. Remember that network building does not necessarily mean that the problem will be instantly solved. What you are trying to elicit are suggestions about where the answer lies. It might be in a book, an organization, or a person not present in the room. Very rarely will someone come up with an impossible problem. Perhaps there is no instant solution, but audience participants can offer moral or emotional support. If nothing else, offer and invite others to carry the person's request to other networks and other individuals.

The Secret of a Good Workshop: Get Out of the Way

Almost any audience composed of people over the age of 12 years old will find ways to be mutually useful if given permission to talk to each other. An amazing amount can be accomplished with a minimum of structure. Your hardest tasks will be to move the workshop along without screaming yourself hoarse over the cheerful bedlam and, more seriously, to convince eager participants that more structure will not necessarily increase the quality or frequency of useful connections. When in doubt, be quiet, and let participants talk to each other. Finally, try to book your room past the official end of the workshop. It is not unusual for participants to stay hours past the closing remarks!

A Handout for Network-Building Workshops

What Is the Art of Network Building?

- A network is a collection of useful relationships.

- The art of networking is the art of exchanging useful ideas and information among individuals in a network for the purpose of mutual benefit.

- The art of network building is designing, building, and maintaining these networks of relationships.

The Five Rules of Networking

1. Be useful to the other person on her terms and allow her to be useful to you.

2. Maintain a balance between giving and taking. Avoid loading other people down with too much data, exploiting other people, or not letting other people be useful to you.

3. Listen! Think about what the other person is saying, not what you are going to say. Seek out people you don't agree with and listen to them.

4. Ask questions as if you assume the other person is going to give you new information.

5. Don't assume who can help you. The least likely person can have the answer to your question and you can be useful to the least likely person.

Other Useful Tips

1. Being useful is not the same as taking care of someone. Networking is about information and idea exchange for mutual benefit; if you try to do too much for other people, you can both undermine their independence and exhaust yourself.

2. The person who consistently refuses assistance can be as boring as the person who always seems to need help. Networking is a transaction and thrives on balance.

3. It is perfectly acceptable to say "no thanks."

4. It may take some time to demonstrate to some people that your desire to ask questions is not an attempt on your part to punish them or put them down, particularly if they grew up in a household where questions were discouraged.

5. Some people think networking is finding the right person and extracting information from him or her. But true networking is learning how to exchange useful information with anyone.

Identifying Your Own Networks

Personal networks: relatives; friends; neighbors; parents of your children's friends; tradespeople and service people; school teachers; hobby and sports club members; friends from personal, religious, and political activities.

Professional networks: colleagues at your current and previous jobs; your peers at other organizations; politicians and appointed officials; members of the media; librarians; clergy; members of professional associations and community groups; members of citizens' groups; private citizens; academics, researchers, and members of thinktanks; property owners, including ranchers, developers, and farmers; business owners and developers.

And how about . . . salespeople, police officers, receptionists and secretaries at other agencies, postal carriers, the kid next door, the person in front of you in line at the grocery store, the person next to you on the plane or bus, your waiter or waitress, your worst enemy, your best friend.

The people most overlooked: your parents, people you have already made up your mind about, people you are in awe of, people you were told about years ago, people you don't know, people who make less money than you or who don't have your education or credentials, and those with superior education and credentials.

Cultivating the Art
of Network Building

1. Invest in your network. Keep a tickler file of people in your personal and professional networks, and call one person each week.

2. Before you try to solve a problem yourself, ask yourself if you couldn't use this as an opportunity to ask someone else for help.

3. Networking is not the same as archiving. The smallest piece of paper or shortest phone call is often the best. Printing endless, thick directories or enormous newsletters, having daily meetings, or sending long computer documents can be boring and counterproductive. Focus on the result you want to achieve and strive to use the fewest bytes of data to send and record the information to achieve the result.

4. The simplest acts of civility and kindness do wonders to build and maintain a professional network. If it is not already automatic for you to say "please" and "thank you" to *everyone*, practice until it is. Smile and take time to acknowledge everyone in the office. In meetings, make introductions for everyone, including secretaries and the person cleaning up. Excellent manners are the mark of an excellent communicator.

5. Choose your hardest question and ask the next 10 people you talk with, no matter who they are, if they have an answer.

6. One productive hour of collecting names, addresses, and phone numbers can equal 20 hours of follow-through. Remember that the next time you are picking up brochures at a conference.

7. Set an example in your office. Be useful and let other people be useful to you.

8. Activate a bulletin board for office professional and personal networking. Get rid of dated items and actively solicit new items.

9. Everyone occasionally hides behind memos and the printed page. Many times a personal phone call or meeting is more effective than a form letter.

Appendix B

Mapping an Array of Alliances Built by Networking

The following illustrates how a local, ad hoc group of parents, teachers, community activists, and artists "just sort of came together" over a 12-year period to bring to life a magnet school for the arts in the public school system.

Many of the people putting this special school program together met through these networks of friends, colleagues, and neighbors. Jan Johnson, a community activist, master gardener, parent, and inventor, lives with her husband in an inner-city neighborhood in Denver. She has had children in both public and private schools. In tracing the linkages among the participants in the magnet school network, Johnson described the kinds of networks of people she might call on in one day to solve a problem related to her own school and neighborhood activities. Notice that very few of the participants in these collections of people and commitments are directly related to schools or school personnel, except as parents.

1. Neighborhood crime fighters

   These include local police officials and those in the city who are committed to ending drug traffic in their neighborhoods. Some of these people make their living dealing with drug and crime issues; others are volunteer citizens whose neighborhoods are under siege by gangs and drug dealers.

2. City zoning officials

   Johnson and her husband, a lawyer, have helped spearhead a

controversial program using zoning laws to have crack houses declared a public nuisance. City officials who are used to dealing with barking dogs and abandoned cars are being forced to deal with absentee landlords of buildings where cocaine is sold to school children.

3.   Local investigative media people

A front-page story in the local paper and the chance to explain their work on radio talk shows has introduced Johnson to radio, television, and newspaper reporters. She keeps in touch by means of phone calls and a newsletter.

4.   Computer technology friends

These are small-business computer users, people Johnson has met through years of business and nonprofit work.

5.   Hispanic community

Sometimes having powerful connections with an allied group of people means having one strong contact in the group. Through a longtime friend who is politically active in the Hispanic community, Johnson has connections she can use.

When asked to name the key person who had started the art school project, Johnson named a Hispanic parent and community activist. This remarkable woman, she said, who lived in a welfare project with the highest crime rate in the city, was able to finish a college education while raising a family. Her dream to start an arts magnet school was fueled by her desire that the school system would support and foster the creativity of children.

6.   Neighborhood organization members

These groups are more formal in structure and often have traditional officers and agendas. Structure allows for credibility with the legal system and continuity to help give neighbors some ownership and pride in the community. In Johnson's city, there are over 140 such neighborhood groups, usually organized around political districts recognized by the city government.

7.   Politicians and bureaucrats

Elected and appointed officials, from the governor's office on down, know Johnson and her work. The fact that these public servants seem to work at cross purposes apparently does not deter Johnson; she has the patience to keep communicating.

8. Union connections

Johnson's husband is a talented performer who once headed the local musician's union. The contacts in the union organizations are the people who know her spouse, but Johnson has built her own personal network with people she has met through formal meetings and parties. The spouses of people who know each other through some affiliation, she points out, tend to network together.

9. Music community members

The music community is another place where Johnson has built her own network with performers and their spouses and families.

10. Psychologists and mental health workers

Through her husband's law practice, which specializes in children's issues such as abuse and guardianship, Johnson has contacts with a variety of behavioral experts.

11. Multiple sclerosis connections

After decades of misdiagnosis, Johnson has become a lay expert in her disease. She recently received a videotape describing a new treatment; the contact came from a person she had met through one of her crime prevention activities. Johnson reports that such serendipitous happenings are one of the rewards she receives for being a good networker.

12. Mothers of her daughters' friends

Her relationship with these parents has strengthened since they discovered that they share a concern about the middle school their children are attending next year. Johnson and the other parents are now banding together to locate educational options.

Johnson identified all of these networks "off the top of her head" in only a few minutes. Her brief list makes it obvious where the energy and interest originated to create the arts school.

Appendix C

Resources

Books

Contemporary Information and Communication Theory

These books were written by some of the leading network and communication theorists. They range from sociological studies of family networks in Europe and Africa to some of the more influential books on computers and technology.

Boissevain, Jeremy, *Friends of Friends: Networks, Manipulators and Coalitions* (New York: St. Martin's Press, Inc., 1974).

Network building as pull, push, politics, and intimidation in several European societies. The stories are interesting and informative, but the author's attitude is a little cynical; he neglects to talk about network building as a means for personal growth and exploration.

Kurjo, Sabine, and Ian McNeill, *Only Connect: The Art and Technology of Networking for Personal and Global Transformation* (London: Turning Points Press, 1988).

An example of how an activist in another culture uses network building as a tool for social change.

Lipnack, Jessica, and Jeffrey Stamps, *Networking: The First Report* (Garden City, NY: Doubleday and Company, Inc., 1982).

The first major popular work on the sociology of network building. The authors focus on those networks that occur in formal organizations, such as clubs, liberal social action groups, and professional associations. The directory is comprehensive, but out of date. See their listing under The Networking Institute in this appendix for more information about their current activities.

Markuson, Barbara Evans, and Blanche Woolls, editors, *Networks for Networkers: Critical Issues in Cooperative Library Development* (New York: Neal-Schuman Publishers, Inc., 1980).

Most of the information in these essays concerns the computerization and connecting of library collections. It is interesting to compare the difference between the information that professionals considered necessary in the late 1970s and what has actually been put in place. A must for school media specialists.

Paulos, John Allen, *Innumeracy: Mathematical Illiteracy and Its Consequences* (New York: Vintage Books, 1988).

A very funny book on probability, with some straightforward explanations that show why the amazing coincidences of network building are not so amazing, but are grounded in well-known mathematical principles.

Pilisuk, Marc, and Susan Hillier Parks, *The Healing Web: Social Networks and Human Survival* (Hanover, NH: University Press of New England, 1986).

A major work in the field of network building. It demonstrates what most peoples have known for generations, which is that personal connections can make a measurable difference in the quality of life.

Rosnow, Ralph L., and Gary Alan Fine, *Rumor and Gossip: The Social Psychology of Hearsay* (New York: Elsevier Scientific Publishing Company, Inc., 1976).

A product of the post-Nixon, Vietnam era of skepticism and unrest. The information on rumor control in institutions is very good.

Roszak, Theodore, *The Cult of Information: The Folklore of Computers and the True Art of Thinking* (New York: Pantheon Books, 1986).

A strong antidote for the thinking in some schools that computers will solve everything. The antibusiness bias is strident at times.

Welch, Mary Scott, *Networking: The Great New Way for Women to Get Ahead* (New York: Harcourt Brace Jovanovich, Inc., 1980).

One of the network-building classics. The information about career building and job hunting, although aimed at women in corporations, is applicable to any working adult.

Wurman, Richard Saul, *Information Anxiety* (New York: Doubleday, 1989).

A popular management book about coping with information overload, with amusing stories about the growth of data businesses.

Volunteerism and Charity

The following books describe some of the opportunities and challenges for those who would serve, either in direct action with other individuals or in support of existing institutions.

Dass, Ram, and Paul Gorman, *How Can I Help? Stories and Reflections on Service* (New York: Alfred A. Knopf, Inc., 1987).

Valuable insights into the challenges of cross-cultural communication and how giving affects both the giver and the receiver. A terrific cure for the blues, particularly when you feel your small efforts are wasted.

Driver, David E., *The Good Heart Book, A Guide to Volunteering* (Chicago: Noble Press, Inc., 1989).

Solid facts about how to improve any volunteer effort. Includes a good national directory.

Elgin, Duane, *Voluntary Simplicity: Towards a Way of Life That Is Outwardly Simple, Inwardly Rich* (New York: William Morrow and Company, Inc., 1981).

Another classic, with useful information about mutual aid. It has a new relevance in our age of environmental concerns. This book started as a small, self-published effort and was acquired by a major publisher when word of its success spread by means of person-to-person networking.

Greenleaf, Robert K., *Teacher As Servant: A Parable* (New York: Paulist Press, 1979).

A simple fable about a professor who decides to create a project to transform society, by demonstrating to students how to become effective leaders in a variety of institutions in both the private and public sectors. For educational professionals, the most important part of the book has to do with how one student began a process that changed the trustees of his college into an effective team.

————, *Servant Leadership: A Journey into the Nature of Legitimate Power and Greatness* (New York: Paulist Press, 1977).

A classic in management, with a strong feel for what motivates the best in people. One section is devoted to change in the educational community.

McClelland, Susan, with Susan McClelland Prescott, *"If There's Anything I Can Do . . .": An Easy Guide to Showing You Care* (Gainesville, FL: Triad Publishing Company, 1990).

If you had a sassy, literate, and loving aunt to tell you what to do when a friend or relative was in need, she would be a lot like Susan McClelland. Much good "networking" starts with people's relationships during hard times, and McClelland and her co-author niece have specific ideas about to handle everything from visits to the hospital to emotional support during a financial crisis.

Children as Network Builders and Communicators

If you have any doubts about the ability of children to be involved in community life in a meaningful way, these books should dispel your fears. They offer terrific ideas for fundraising projects and wise insights into motivating children to be creative, disciplined, fiscally responsible, and cooperative.

Barkin, Carol, and Elizabeth James, *Jobs for Kids: The Guide to Having Fun and Making Money* (New York: Lothrop, Lee and Shepard, Inc., 1990).

Good ideas for projects that students can do in the community.

Drew, Bonnie, and Noel Drew, *Kid Biz: Year-Round Money Making Projects for Junior Entrepreneurs* (Austin, TX: Eakin Press, 1990).

This contains similar information to *Jobs for Kids*, but is more formally structured. Both are inexpensive paperbacks and deserve to be in every school library.

Hess, Karl, *Capitalism for Kids: Growing Up To Be Your Own Boss* (Wilmington, DE: Enterprise Publishing, Inc., 1987).

The first of a proposed series of books on philosophy, logic, and problem solving for children by the same author. An excellent book about respecting the intelligence and integrity of children and how adults can foster fiscal responsibility, initiative, creativity, and self-discipline among children.

Professional and Personal Development

Compared with other professions, there is a surprising lack of good literature on professional development for teachers that focuses on personal and career growth, rather than on the craft and content of teaching. Included here are books from other disciplines, notably business and corporate wellness, that can prove helpful to educators.

Beale, Lucy, and Rick Fields, *The Win-Win Way: The New Approach Transforming American Business and Life* (Orlando, FL: Harcourt Brace Jovanovich, 1987).

The authors remind business people to cooperate more. This little book gave the world the phrase "win-win."

The Bradley Commission on History in Schools, *Historical Literacy, the Case for History in American Education* (Boston: Houghton Mifflin, 1989).

Chapter 14, "Obstacles Teachers Confront: What Needs to Change," contains a wonderful description of the burden of the present-day school teacher.

Fisher, Roger, and William Ury, *Getting to Yes: Negotiating without Giving In* (Boston: Houghton Mifflin, 1983).

A genuine classic and perhaps the best book on communicating with people during difficult times. Written by participants in the Harvard Negotiation Project, this book has transformed the way many institutions conduct labor negotiations. Contains priceless advice for network builders about the art of the transaction.

Levine, Sarah L., *Promoting Adult Growth in Schools* (Needham Heights, MA: Allyn and Bacon, 1989).

This excellent book follows several teachers through their careers over several years and notes how, through professional intervention, they were able to make changes in their careers and their lives. The author offers several current models in psychology with applications to school personnel in every stage of their careers.

Loehr, James E., and Peter J. McLaughlin, *Mentally Tough: The Principles of Winning at Sports Applied to Winning in Business* (New York: M. Evans and Company, Inc., 1986).

Good advice on dealing with work-related stress.

McGee-Cooper, Ann, *You Don't Have To Go Home from Work Exhausted: The Energy Engineering Approach* (Dallas, TX: Bowen and Rogers, 1990).

An encyclopedic approach to how to keep your energy up and your day under control. The best book on coping with institutional burnout, although some of the theory is not scientifically based.

Von Oech, Roger, *A Whack on the Side of the Head: How To Unlock Your Mind for Innovation* (New York: Perennial Library, 1986).

Another classic on creativity, with exercises that could be applied in the classroom or the teachers' lounge with equal success.

Periodicals

Several categories of magazines are useful for building networks. If you are like most professionals, you probably subscribe to so many journals in your own field that you are unable to read them thoroughly. You skim the table of contents, circle a few articles, and consign the rest to oblivion. The articles you like, you clip to do something about later. If you are well organized, you might even file them or make copies to send to friends.

These are wonderful archival habits, but are not necessarily the best in terms of network building. Consider changing the kind of magazines you subscribe to and changing how you use the information you find in them.

1. Start by ruthlessly winnowing your subscriptions to the few magazines you seem to make the time to read as soon as they arrive at your door, and drop the ones you receive because you "ought to" read them but you never do.

2. Ask colleagues and members of your networks what they read and why. Look at magazines and newsletters that cover business (*Forbes, INC.*), science (*Discover*), computers (*Byte*), current events and culture (*Insight, World Monitor, Whole Earth Review*), management (*Harvard Business Review*), and the so-called "think" magazines (*Mother Jones, Reason, National Review, The Nation, Harper's, Atlantic Monthly*).

3. Choose one or two new magazines each year to try for one year; pick one that is outside your field and one that reflects a political outlook different from your own.

4. Look at and read the magazines your students read.

The following magazines and newsletters were chosen either for their useful tidbits of eclectic information, their excellent use of the network-building model, or because they contain interesting and iconoclastic information for the school professional. Additionally, most of the organizations listed below have their own publications. Write for current subscription rates.

Catalyst
332 S. Michigan Avenue
Suite 500
Chicago, IL 60604-9863
(312) 427-4830

Offers extraordinary continuous coverage of the Chicago school reform experiment, including an ongoing diary of the thoughts of participants in the councils and commentary by everyone from the superintendent of schools to parents and students. Edited by professional journalists.

The Link
c/o The Access Center
3040 W. Walnut
Chicago, IL 60612
(312) 638-8700

Published quarterly by Catholic Charities, focusing on local, regional, and national charitable issues. Contains contact information for dozens of organizations and resources.

Skipping Stones
Aprovecho Institute
80574 Hazelton Road
Cottage Grove, OR 97424
(503) 942-9434

A multi-ethnic, nonprofit children's magazine to encourage cooperation, creativity, and celebration of cultural and environmental richness. "We accept artwork and original writings in every language and from all ages."

Spacefaring Gazette: A Journal for Space Development
P.O. Box 2719
Oakland, CA 94602

A bimonthly publication on space exploration and colonization.

Organizations

This list of organizations is downplayed for several reasons. First, the most cost-effective network building begins with the people you already know in your own immediate community. Making connections with network organizations in other states or with successful national clearinghouses can be useful. But it may make less sense to spend valuable time and money collecting information from an educational foundation a thousand miles away than to call the education editor of your community weekly or the state librarian for local suggestions.

Second, if you want to be credible to your colleagues, network building needs to start at home. People will be more likely to promote your efforts if they believe you practice what you preach. You might have someone in your personal web of friendship who is nationally known in her field, but whom you tend to discount because you know her too well to be impressed by her credentials.

Third, building support networks starts with the activity of building relationships; "doing" is different than "talking" and "reading." The fine threads of respect and reciprocity that bind a community together in a healthy manner are spun by working with people. This does not mean you must never go out of your community for resources. It just means that if one of your major goals is to strengthen the support your school receives locally, you must start locally.

Remember the etiquette of contacting organizations:

1   Let them know who you are and where you found out about them.

2.   Describe what you are trying to accomplish; be as specific and succinct as possible.

3.   Ask for introductory material and ask if there is any cost involved.

4.   Ask what you can do for them and offer at least one specific suggestion.

5.   When humanly possible, thank them for what they have sent, pay them something if you can, and give them some feedback.

Educational Organizations

Information on these organizations is quoted directly from their literature.

African Studies Association
Credit Union Building
Emory University
Atlanta, GA 30322

Resources on Africa for educators, media specialists, community and business groups.

Alliance for Achievement Network
Suite 402
1603 S. Michigan Avenue
Chicago, IL 60616
(312) 427-1692

Membership is open to any school, public or private, that wishes to contribute to its effectiveness by building a strong, value-based school community. Principal submits application. Call or write for current information. Published *Alliance for Achievement*, a handbook on building the value-based school community.

Alliance for Parental Involvement in Education, Inc.
P.O. Box 59
East Chatham, NY 12060-0059
518-392-6900

A national nonprofit organization to encourage and assist parental involvement in education. Several publications. Write for current price list.

Association for Experiential Education
University of Colorado
Box 249
Boulder, CO 80309
(303) 492-1547

An international organization of members committed to furthering experiential-based teaching and learning.

Institute for Independent Education, Inc.
P.O. Box 42571
Washington, DC 20015

A national network of minority, urban-based private schools. Publications, workshops, conferences, research.

The International Society for Intercultural Education, Training, and Research
733 15th Street, NW
Suite 900
Washington, DC 20005
(202) 737-5000

A multi-disciplinary, multi-cultural international networking society dealing with intercultural issues in the world today.

KidsArt
P.O. Box 274
Mt. Shasta, CA 96067
(916) 926-5076

An arts organization for children, educators, and parents providing free catalogs of art supplies and crafts materials. *KidsArt* is the organization's magazine with information on art projects, educational art information, and ideas for projects outside the classroom.

League for Innovation in the Community College
25431 Cabot Road
Suite 204
Laguna Hills, CA 92653
(714) 855-0710

A nonprofit educational consortium of resourceful community colleges organized to stimulate experimentation and innovation in all areas of community college development. Stiff membership requirements. Active, participatory program.

National Association of School Nurses, Inc.
Lamplighter Lane
P.O. Box 1300
Scarborough, ME 04074
(207) 883-2117

Promotes excellence in school health.

National Coalition of Alternative Community Schools
58 Schoolhouse Road
Summertown, TN 38483
(615) 964-3670

A national coalition of schools, groups, and individuals. Please send at least $1 for more information about publications, directories, and services.

National Community Education Association
801 N. Fairfax Street
Suite 209
Alexandria, VA 22314
(703) 683-6232

To promote parent and community involvement in public education; the formation of community partnerships to address community needs; and the expansion of lifelong learning opportunities for community residents of all ages and educational backgrounds. A source of many classic books. Write for current price list and services.

USA Toy Library Association
2719 Broadway Avenue
Evanston, IL 60201
(708) 864-8240

A national networking association for toy libraries. Published *The Toy Librarian Operator's Manual*, a primer on the subject.

Other Organizations and Businesses

These organizations either support network building through consulting services, software, books, etc., or run interesting national networks.

Alliance for Cultural Democracy
P.O. Box 7591
Minneapolis, MN 55407

Supports community cultural participation. Publications, conferences, national networking.

Association for Volunteer Administration
P.O. Box 4584
Boulder, CO 80306

A professional association for those working in the field of volunteer management. Publications, conferences, and support.

International Network for Social Network Analysis (INSNA)
c/o Alvin W. Wolfe, Ph.D.
Center for Applied Anthropology
University of South Florida
Tampa, FL 33620-8100

The international network linking network analysts in several academic disciplines, including education. Publications, analysis, and conferences.

Metasystems Design Group, Inc.
2000 N. 15th Street
Suite 103
Arlington, VA 22201
(703) 243-6622

Computer-supported cooperative work. Their software, Caucus™, supports IRIS, a national online computer conferencing tool for teachers and educators.

The Networking Institute, Inc.
505 Waltham Street
West Newton, MA 02165
(617) 965-3340

Consulting services, educational seminars, and workshops to small groups and large organizations. Will help a group or organization create a handbook to capture the group's knowledge base. Write for current list of books and publications.

SRM Corporation
2653 W. 32nd Avenue
Denver, CO 80211
(303) 433-7163

Provides comprehensive network mapping and interpretative services for schools, agencies, businesses, and citizen groups. Over 20 years in community mediation work.

TRANET
Box 567
Rangeley, ME 04970
(207) 864-2252

An international networking organization with no political or governmental ties. Publishes a bimonthly newsletter and directory of, by, and for people who are participating in transformation and adopting alternative technologies.

Index